Baby Girls

D0168805

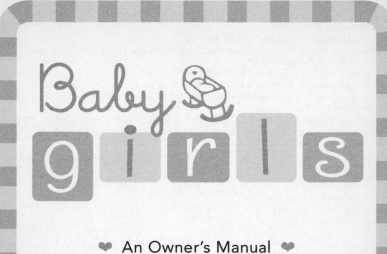

Baby girls

❤ An Owner's Manual ❤

THERESA FOY DIGERONIMO, M.ED.

Foreword by Stephen E. Muething

A Perigee Book

THE BERKLEY PUBLISHING GROUP
Published by the Penguin Group
Penguin Group (USA) Inc.
375 Hudson Street, New York, New York 10014, USA
Penguin Group (Canada), 90 Eglinton Avenue East, Suite 700, Toronto, Ontario M4P 2Y3, Canada
(a division of Pearson Penguin Canada Inc.)
Penguin Books Ltd., 80 Strand, London WC2R 0RL, England
Penguin Group Ireland, 25 St. Stephen's Green, Dublin 2, Ireland (a division of Penguin Books Ltd.)
Penguin Group (Australia), 250 Camberwell Road, Camberwell, Victoria 3124, Australia
(a division of Pearson Australia Group Pty. Ltd.)
Penguin Books India Pvt. Ltd., 11 Community Centre, Panchsheel Park, New Delhi—110 017, India
Penguin Group (NZ), Cnr. Airborne and Rosedale Roads, Albany, Auckland 1310, New Zealand
(a division of Pearson New Zealand Ltd.)
Penguin Books (South Africa) (Pty.) Ltd., 24 Sturdee Avenue, Rosebank, Johannesburg 2196,
South Africa
Penguin Books Ltd., Registered Offices: 80 Strand, London WC2R 0RL, England

Copyright © 2005 by Literary Productions
Text design by Tiffany Estreicher
Cover art and design by Liz Sheehan

PRINTING HISTORY
Perigee trade paperback edition / December 2005

PERIGEE is a registered trademark of Penguin Group (USA) Inc.
The "P" design is a trademark belonging to Penguin Group (USA) Inc.

Library of Congress Cataloging-in-Publication Data

DiGeronimo, Theresa Foy.
    Baby girls : a complete guide to your daughter's first 18 months / by Theresa Foy
DeGeronimo ; foreword by Stephen E. Meuthing.
        p.   cm.
    "A Perigee Book."
    "Developed by Literary Productions."
    Includes bibliographical references.
    ISBN 0-399-53211-0
    1. Infant girls—Health and hygiene.   2. Infant girls—Care.   I. Title.

RJ61.D562   2005
649'.133—dc22

                                              2005043253

PRINTED IN THE UNITED STATES OF AMERICA

10   9   8   7   6   5   4   3   2   1

Contents

Two

Your Infant Daughter:
From Birth Through Three Months

Three

Watch Her Grow:
Your Daughter from Four to Seven Months

Four

On the Move: Your Daughter From Eight to Eleven Months

Five

Toddler Time: Your Daughter From Twelve to Eighteen Months . . . and Beyond

Baby Girls

Foreword

It seems like just yesterday when my wife, Meg, and I had our first baby girl. Little Amy was born on November 4, 1982, and weighed 8 pounds, 4 ounces. At the time, I was a starving undergraduate at the University of Notre Dame, and knew very little about kids. And having a daughter was quite an eye-opening experience, especially since I came from a family of seven boys.

In the very beginning, like most parents, my biggest emotion was *fear*—fear of the unknown and fear that I would make a mistake in raising her. To be honest, the fact that she was a girl wasn't that big of a deal, at least not in the first month or so. But before long, as Amy moved through the toddler years, my wife and I were constantly talking about how different girls are from boys in so many ways.

Right from the start, I was waiting for my girl to show an interest in sports and what I call "rough-and-tumble" play. But she wanted nothing to do with that. Amy liked soft caresses and hugs. She loved being held close, but hated pushing and play wrestling.

No question about it, I sure could have used a copy of *Baby Girls* to help get me through these times.

Our second daughter, Molly, came along four years later, closely followed by our first son, Ted. Once again, my wife and I began to marvel at how different Ted was compared to our two girls. We wondered aloud whether boys could really be so dissimilar from girls. The answer, of course, was yes.

Granted, in those early years, I was just finishing up my studies in medical school, so all of my observations were as a parent, not as a seasoned pediatrician. Now, after twelve years in private practice and as associate director of clinical services at Cincinnati Children's Hospital Medical Center, I can assure you from a medical perspective that there are some big differences between boys and girls, from their health to the way they act.

To begin with, girls are less likely to be born premature. They are less apt to have attention deficit disorder; their personalities are different; they have smaller appetites, are more cool-headed, and enter puberty much sooner than boys. You can even see these disparities in such areas as toilet training. Girls are much more open to having people in the room while they learn how to use the potty, while boys like their privacy. And when it comes to playing sports, girls are twice as likely to have blow-out knee injuries as boys. The list goes on and on, but I think you get the idea. These differences only increase as they grow older.

I always tell parents that raising a child is the most important job they'll ever have. Since we're all poorly prepared for this awesome responsibility, it would be nice if we could have a specific owner's manual to guide us through the parenting process. The book you are holding in your hands goes a long way toward fitting this bill in a way that's quite unique from anything else out there.

In the pages that follow, Theresa Foy DiGeronimo—a parenting expert in her own right—will guide you through what you need to know as you raise your beautiful girl from birth through the early toddler years. In addition to presenting you with the latest research and medical findings, Theresa will share her personal experiences in raising her own daughter with you. (She also has two boys, so she's lived through these differences firsthand.)

Knowing the basics will go a long way toward making you the best parent you can be. This book will show you how to care for your girl, how to feed her, and how to keep her safe. It will also help you to understand your daughter's own individuality, the nuances of her body and personality, and fantastic ways to keep her happy. By understanding her own unique traits—and how girls differ from boys—you'll have a solid head start in doing the greatest job of all.

Before you get started on this journey, let me leave you with a bit of parting advice. First, whether you're still expecting or have already welcomed your baby girl into the world, don't be surprised if you're a little scared. It's perfectly normal to feel like you may be in over your head, while fearing you'll do something wrong. Almost every new parent feels that way. I sure did.

The important thing is for you to take care of your daughter the best way you know how, and to also take care of your partner. You're in this together and will need each other now more than ever to get through the experience. Slow down your lives, and take everything day by day. You're going to be exhausted, especially in your girl's first few months. Then, as time goes by, you'll begin to realize that you're getting the hang of this parenting thing. You'll be more at ease, and you'll sleep better at night.

If you already have a son, and this is your first girl, I'd add this bit of advice: Hang on! It's going to be a much different ride. Yes, you will have to change your parenting style to adjust to your daughter's unique needs. Fortunately, a lot of the basics in the early years are the same, so it won't be quite as scary as it was the first time around. But it will be different, and this book will help you to deal with that.

The good news is that early successes in parenting build on each other. As a result, if you are able to understand, accept, and deal with these smaller differences now, you are bound to be better prepared to handle the big stuff that's sure to come as your daughter grows older. After all, the teenage years will be here before you know it!

So get ready for what's bound to be a wonderful journey as you raise your little girl. Remember, it's okay to make mistakes, and the more you know and understand about your daughter going in, the better you'll be able to cope with the many adventures you are about to encounter.

Stephen E. Muething, M.D.
Associate Director of Clinical Services, Cincinnati Children's Hospital
Medical Center
Assistant Professor, Pediatrics, University of Cincinnati

Introduction

I have raised my daughter through the ups and downs of baby-hood and can tell you for certain that a baby girl is very special in-deed. She is a squeezable delight of giggles and kisses, a tyrannical foot-stomper, and a moody sulker. She is a gift with no match, and at the end of every day, a true blessing. But there's so much to learn about little girls, and so little time.

In this book, we'll begin the exploration by mapping out what you need to know in your daughter's earliest years, from setting up the nursery to selecting just the right foods. Then we'll talk about things like routine home health care, good sleep habits (for your daughter and for you!), the process of bonding, and expected physical growth.

As we move through the years, you'll learn, how to tame a tem-per tantrum, and effective ways to deal with such conditions as uri-nary tract infections and weight problems (both of which are much more common in girls).

As both a mother and the author of numerous parenting books on a variety of topics, I'll open the doors to giving you a better understanding of just how and why girls are so different from boys, including the latest research into this topic from the many recognized experts I have turned to for advice and guidance.

As you'll see, there are sound scientific studies explaining why girls and boys are quite different. You'll discover that many aspects of being female thought to be merely stereotypical are actually based on facts. For instance, girls really are less active and aggressive and they do talk more than boys. They seem to be biologically wired to prefer dolls over trucks. They are often not as good at math as boys, but they tend to have far fewer learning disabilities and developmental problems.

Baby Girls: An Owner's Manual brings you into the world of sugar and spice and everything nice, while examining the physical, cognitive, and emotional makeup of girls to help you to better understand your newly formed XX chromosome miracle. It gives you information, tips, and advice about pressing parenting issues and concerns—while always keeping an eye on the world from your little girl's point of view. At the end of each chapter, you'll find quotes from other parents just like you, who share their feelings about raising a baby girl—the good, the bad, and the precious.

While this book is divided by age range, you may find it interesting to read the book from start to finish so you can get a complete picture of all the factors that influence the development of a female from birth to around eighteen months. Then, refer to each section over and over again as your daughter moves through the first critical stages of childhood. You'll come away not only with better parenting skills, but also with answers to such questions as,

"Why does she always act that way?" and "Is it really normal for girls to do that?"

By the time you're through, you'll have a much better understanding of what girls are made of, along with the knowledge of what you can do to prepare for this new lifelong adventure.

One

It's A Baby Girl!

Through the marvels of modern medicine, you may be preparing for your baby girl before you've even given birth. How wonderful to know your daughter, to feel her high kicks, and to call her by name before the two of you have formally met. Or, you may be reading this book after you've held your daughter, kissed her forehead, and wondered in a panic: *Now what!?* Either way, here's some information to get you going on the right track.

In this chapter, we'll explore some of the basics you need to prepare for even before bringing your daughter home from the hospital. In a moment, we'll talk about selecting a doctor and getting your baby girl's room set up. But first we'll discuss one of the most basic decisions you'll have to make (and also one of the most enjoyable): finding the right name for your bundle of joy.

A Rose by Any Other Name . . .
Naming Your Daughter

I gave my daughter the strong Irish name of Colleen—meaning "little girl" in Gaelic (or so I'm told). My side of the family is solidly Irish on both sides, and so it seemed unfair that this strong heritage be lost in the last name DiGeronimo. My solution was met with raised eyebrows, though my bonnie lass has carried her Irish/Italian name without trouble or incident. Indeed, there is no law limiting what you can call your daughter. Comedian and civil rights leader Dick Gregory gave his twins the middles names of Inte and Gration. Cher and Sonny Bono named their daughter Chastity Sun. Mia Farrow and Andre Previn chose Lark Song and Summer Song for their daughters. So if you feel like being creative, there's nothing stopping you (except perhaps good judgment).

Until the 1700s, the issue of naming a daughter in America was not cause for pause. Like their brothers, girls were named after a relative. The firstborn was named after her father's mother; the second born after her mother's mother; the third born after her mother herself; and later daughters after the mother's and father's sisters. In fact, if you decide to name your daughter after her mother and add "Junior" to her name, you won't be breaking new ground. In the 1700s in New England, it was quite common to find references to "Elizabeth Smith, Jr." on legal wills and deeds. This cultural tradition changed in the 1800s when families began giving their daughters names outside the family tree.

Dr. Cleveland Kent Evans of the American Name Society says that since that time, girls have been given more varied and fanciful names than boys. Like fashions, female names are now worn for show, to differentiate the bearer from other females. And these names change in popularity rather quickly. There will be four Stephanies in first grade one year and then four Jessicas the next— upsetting all the parents who thought they had found a unique name for their daughter! In general, parents of girls often place "unique" at the top of their name-criteria list. In fact, the most popular names given to females each year are not truly popular at all. Dr. Evans notes that in the 1990s, the top fifty names for girls were given to less than 40 percent of the newborns.

Some parents of daughters commit to female names that fit their infants without projecting the name into adulthood. For this reason more women than men will have names that seem inappropriate for adults ("Pixie" comes to mind). Female names also are more likely

MOST POPULAR FEMALE NAMES

According to the most recent report by the Social Security Administration, the most popular female names were:

1. Emily	5. Hannah	8. Ashley
2. Emma	6. Abigail	9. Samantha
3. Madison	7. Isabella	10. Elizabeth
4. Olivia		

You can find more information about popular baby names online from the Social Security Administration at:
http://www.ssa.gov/OACT/babynames

to be "modern" than male names. It is quite common, for example, for little boys to have the same names as men over age forty (such as Bob, Mike, or Joe), but not so for females. Names common in women over forty such as Linda, Nancy, Mary, Barbara, and Kathy are today rarely given to little girls; they are considered too "old."

QUICK CHECKLIST FOR CHOOSING YOUR DAUGHTER'S NAME

As you're tossing around possible names for your baby girl, keep these tips in mind to help you make a decision you and your child can live with for many years to come:

- ☐ **Say it out loud.** Does the first name and your last name flow nicely and sound good together? Do they bang into each other and trip up the tongue? Or do they make you laugh (like Sadie Faydie)?

- ☐ **Does the name you're thinking of have a nickname?** If you don't like the nickname, stay away from the proper name—once kids reach school, you may lose control of what the other children call your daughter. Gabriella can become Gabby whether you like it or not.

- ☐ **Check out the initials.** I planned to name my firstborn Matthew Adam, but then realized his initials would be M.A.D. and quickly changed my mind.

- ☐ **Consider gender identification.** There are several names and nicknames that can be male or female, such as Sam, or Chris.

REMARKABLE FEMALE NAMES

In his book *Remarkable Names of Real People,* John Train lists hundreds of unusual names for baby girls, some clever, some cruel. How would you like to go through life with these? Orange Marmalade, Ave Maria Klinkenberg, Constant Agony, Hedda Hare, Honor Roll, Imaculada Concepciòn (Immaculate Conception), Iva Odor, and Needa Climax.

If you choose such a name, your child will be plagued with name problems for the rest of her life. My neighbor's daughter arrived for her first day of college to find that her roommate, Chris, was male, requiring a quick reshuffling of room assignments, and much embarrassment for poor Chris.

Your Baby Girl's Doctor

The physician who looks in on your daughter immediately after her birth may not be the one you want to stick with in the long run. Because your daughter's doctor will care for her medical needs from birth to approximately age eighteen, you should choose this long-term relationship carefully.

THINGS TO THINK ABOUT

When choosing your baby's doctor, here are some things to think about:

Pediatrician or Family Practitioner: A pediatrician is a physician who specializes in the development, care, and diseases of children. A family practitioner is a physician with training in many areas of medicine and can be the primary care provider for all members of your family. Both are qualified to care for your daughter. When making the choice, you have to decide if you would like your daughter in the care of someone who has specialized training with babies and children or if you'd like someone who knows and cares for you, too. If your daughter is healthy with no special needs, choose the doctor you are most comfortable with. But if your daughter has any medical problems that require careful monitoring, many families find it best to select a pediatrician with specialized training in childhood illness and their treatment.

Solo or Group Practice: In a solo practice the doctor works alone; group practitioners work with several other doctors in the same office. Both arrangements have their good and bad points. Families who choose the solo practitioner like having one person who really knows the child. This physician tends to remember the child and knows the details of her special needs. The parents get consistent information from one source. On the down side, there's only so much one person can do. If he or she is called out on an emergency, you may end up sitting in the waiting room for hours. If you call with your own emergency while the doctor is on vacation or out of town, your daughter will be seen by a covering doctor whom you may have never met at all. And with only one doctor in the office, it's often difficult to schedule convenient appointments.

Group practitioners come with their own set of advantages and disadvantages. Although you may have a favored doctor among the participating physicians who handles the baby's checkups, when your daughter is sick and needs immediate care, you will see whomever is in the office that day with an opening. But at least this person will be someone you have at least a nodding acquaintance with, who has all your child's records on hand, and who works in an environment that is familiar to your daughter.

Insurance Considerations: If you have insurance you may want to narrow your search by choosing a doctor who participates in your health-care plan. Your provider may have given you a booklet or a website listing all participating doctors in your area. If not, you can call member services and ask for help in locating doctors near you.

Of course you can go out-of-network to a nonparticipating physician, but it will cost you. Unlike most healthy adults who may see a doctor once or twice a year, routine childhood checkups and illnesses are quite frequent and the bills can pile up quickly. Before you sign up with an out-of-network physician, find out exactly how much each checkup will cost you, along with the charges you will pay for emergency and hospital care, that way you can make an informed decision.

Location: It's a good idea to stick close to home. Children commonly need quick emergency treatment for high fevers, deep cuts, and the like. Lengthy trips to a long-distance physician will soon wear you out.

Male or Female: Your infant daughter will not care about the gender of her doctor. But as she grows, this can become an issue. I found that my baby girl was more comfortable and calmer with a female doctor when she was sick or in pain. We have stuck with a female pediatrician ever since. If you choose a group practice, watch how she reacts to a male versus a female doctor and take your cues from that. You can probably specify your preference for a male or female doctor if both are in the practice.

ASK AROUND

As you narrow down your preferences, be sure to ask around for recommendations. A physician may look impressive on paper based on his or her education and position in the medical community, but only those families who rely on a doctor for medical care really know what's equally important—how he or she handles worried parents and sick children.

You might first ask your obstetrician for a reference. (Ask who she uses for her own kids!) Also, talk to friends and family members who have already chosen a doctor for their children. Look for answers to the following:

- ☐ Does your doctor welcome questions?

- ☐ Does she take time to discuss problems and listen to your concerns?

- ☐ Is the office staff pleasant and helpful?

- ☐ How long do you wait in the waiting room? (This becomes a very important consideration when your child is sick and ill-tempered.)

☐ Does the waiting room have a separate area for sick children?

☐ How quickly does he return your calls?

☐ Does your child like the doctor?

Based on all this information, make a list of the top few physicians you might choose and get out and meet them.

TIME FOR AN INTERVIEW

Time is tight at a bustling doctor's office so it's never a good idea to drop in for a "surprise" interview. But if you plan ahead, most physicians will agree to talk with you about their practice. (Many physicians offer half-hour consultations for a nominal charge.) Call each doctor's office and ask if you can set up a potential-patient interview. Some physicians will have time for only a phone conversation. Others will invite you to the office. (If you have to settle for a phone call, be sure to visit the office to look around the waiting area before making your final decision. There's a lot you can learn from the state of cleanliness, organization, and crowding of the office that you can't get over the phone.) The kind of response you get for your request for an interview will perhaps tell you all you need to know about a physician who is too busy, too important, or too disinterested to meet with a new parent.

Use your interview time to ask questions about the practical aspects of the doctor's practice, as well as his or her beliefs and philosophy. For example, you might ask:

HOW TO FIND THE BEST DOCTOR

You can get the names of doctors who are certified by the American Board of Pediatrics from:

• Your local medical society

• A hospital referral service

• The American Academy of Pediatrics, or AAP. Send a self-addressed, stamped envelope to: Pediatric Referral Department, AAP, P.O. Box 927, Elk Grove Village, IL 60009. Be sure to mention which region of the country you're interested in.

☐ What are the office hours? Are you available on weekends? How are emergencies on holidays or middle-of-the-night calls handled?

☐ If this is a group practice, will my child see the same doctor at each checkup?

☐ At what hospital do you have full staff privileges?

☐ Are sick children in the same waiting room with healthy kids waiting for checkups?

☐ Who is your covering doctor when you're not available?

☐ What is your payment and billing policy?

☐ What is your advice about how to handle a crying baby?

☐ If I have trouble breastfeeding, will I be able to call you for help?

The office staff might be able to answer some of the practical questions before your interview, leaving you more time to ask the doctor about her feelings and opinions on child-care matters that are most important to you. The person you choose will care for your child into the teen years, so be sure it is someone you like and trust.

Stocking Up for Your Baby Girl

The list of baby "things" you'll want to buy before your daughter arrives is, of course, endless, but here are a few items that experienced parents say they were glad to have in the house before delivery day.

DIAPERS

You wouldn't be the first parent to bring home a new baby and realize an hour later that you need to buy diapers. If you are using disposable diapers, look for the newborn size with a cutout around the navel. However, don't buy too many because your daughter will quickly outgrow them. They are good for about three weeks at the most while the baby's cord stump is drying out.

If you're using cloth diapers, purchase about six dozen in size large (they can be folded to fit your daughter at each stage of growth). You might also consider buying diaper liners, which absorb small amounts of urine and are then changed easily, without adding another full diaper to the laundry load. You'll also need six diaper wraps or plastic pants and six pairs of diaper pins.

In addition to diapers, you'll also need diapering supplies. Buy a tube of ointment for preventing diaper rash, but make it a small one. You may have to try a brand or two until you find one that works best on your daughter. Many doctors say it's best to stay away from commercial baby wipes when changing a newborn. They have been known to cause harsh reactions on the baby's soft bottom. Stick to sterile cotton balls dipped in warm water for cleanups.

BABY CLOTHES

Little-girl clothes are so cute! We all fall in love with the lacy dresses and bonnets. But I learned the hard way that little girls barely have a chance to go out on the town before they outgrow their infant clothing. It's usually best to leave the buying of fancy frills to relatives and friends. Focus your buying power on a practical day-to-day wardrobe that includes the following:

☐ At least six stretchy, snap-up-the-front, one-piece pajamas with feet. These are the most useful fashion wear for newborns. They live in them!

☐ At least a half-dozen front-snapping tee shirts or one-piece snap-crotch tees.

☐ Another half-dozen pairs of socks or booties. (Booties that tie around the ankle will stay on longer than socks.)

☐ A hat. Whether the weather calls for a wool hat or a sun hat, you'll want to keep your daughter's head covered.

☐ A snowsuit, if you live in a cold region.

HEALTH AND GROOMING AIDS

There are a few items you might want to have on hand when your daughter arrives. The following will take care of any minor health problems in the first few weeks and also keep your daughter well groomed:

Cool-mist Humidifier: Dry air is tough on little nostrils. A cool-mist humidifier will help your daughter breathe easy.

Bulb Syringe: Even with a humidifier in the room, it's likely that your daughter will still get the occasional stuffy nose. Until she learns to blow her nose like the rest of us, the bulb syringe is the best way to remove mucus from a congested nose.

Rectal Thermometer: It will be a while before you can use the family oral thermometer to check your daughter's temperature. The rectal type is a must—either mercury or digital. And pick up some petroleum jelly to coat the thermometer before use for easy insertion.

Rounded-tipped Scissor or Baby Nail Clipper: You'll be amazed how quickly little baby fingernails and toenails grow! The fingernails especially must be kept very short so your daughter won't scratch the delicate skin on her face.

Comb and/or Hairbrush: Adult and big-kid combs and brushes can scratch a newborn's scalp. Get one designed specifically for newborns with soft brush bristles and rounded comb teeth.

BABY MONITOR

An audio baby monitor lets you eavesdrop on your daughter when she is out of sight. It consists of a transmitter that is placed in the baby's room and a portable receiver that can be placed in another room or carried around to hear her cries, sighs, and breathing. Volume is adjustable and some have visual cues, such as red lights that go on when a sound registers.

You might also think about going high-tech with a video monitor. These are available at most baby supply stores and are easy to install and use. They consist of a video camera that you can train on your sleeping baby and a small (4×5") television monitor to keep nearby wherever you are in the house.

These monitors, whether audio or video, can be reassuring devices. They're especially comforting if you're a sound sleeper and

MONITOR WARNING

Baby monitor transmissions can be picked up on cell phones as well as on neighbors' baby monitor receivers. So be careful what you say in the baby's room—many a parent has had an embarrassingly frank conversation before remembering the transmitter was on.

your daughter sleeps in another room, or if you have a large house and want to be alerted when baby wakes from a nap.

BABY BATHTUB

Some folks say that you can bathe an infant in any plastic tub, or in the sink, or in the bathtub with a towel under her to prevent slipping. While this is true, bathing a young baby is a slippery business. That's why a baby bathtub especially molded for infants can be a big help, particularly if you are not practiced in the art of baby handling.

The tub should be made of a plastic heavy enough not to bend under the weight of a full load of water. It should have a plug for draining the water, a slip-resistant bottom, and be shaped to hold your daughter in a semi-upright position on a slip-resistant surface. For a longer period of usefulness, get a tub good for infants or toddlers. Indentations to hold washcloths, soap, and a cup (for rinsing) are nice features.

Whatever you choose, you won't use the tub and submerge your daughter's belly into the water until she is a couple of weeks old and the umbilical cord stump has healed. Until then, you'll just use a washcloth or sponge for daily cleaning. (For more on bathing your daughter, see Chapter 2.)

Safety First

As you're choosing the furniture for your daughter's nursery, here are few tips to help you decorate, keeping style and safety in mind.

CHANGING TABLE

In the first year or so, you'll spend a lot of time changing your daughter's diapers, so a solid and safe changing table is a good investment—and the best way to prevent the backaches you'd otherwise get from bending over to change her diapers while she's on your bed or the floor.

The changing table you choose should have room for storing supplies so you never have to leave your daughter unattended to grab a diaper or ointment. It must also have a safety strap that is easy to use. The U.S. Consumer Product Safety Commission (CPSC) website says that more than 1,300 infants are injured in changing table–related accidents each year. Most of these injuries occur when babies fall from the changing table to the floor. So, look for a good strap and then be sure to use it. (And remember: *Just because you are using the safety straps it does not mean that you can leave your daughter unattended.*)

BABY BED

Your daughter's first bed—whether cradle or crib—is an important purchase. It is the one place she will spend most of her time until she's up on her feet and running. So it's important to make sure it is a safe place—whether bassinet, cradle, or crib.

Bassinet or Cradle: Who can resist the beauty of a lacy bassinet or the polished wood of an infant cradle? Either one is an ideal addition to any nursery. My bassinet was entirely covered with white lace and it had a traditional hooded design. I was very disappointed when after only three weeks my baby grew too long for its diminutive size and was kicking so hard at the sides I worried about its stability. This was probably my first lesson in how quickly our babies grow.

The CPSC warns that the most frequent injury associated with bassinets and cradles involves children falling either when the bottom of the bassinet or cradle breaks, or when it tips over or collapses. Suffocation has also been reported in products that are not structurally sound or when pillows or folded quilts were under the baby.

If you buy a bassinet or cradle, keep these CPSC tips in mind:

☐ Look for one with a sturdy bottom and a wide, stable base.

☐ Follow the manufacturer's guidelines on the appropriate weight and size of baby who can safely use the bassinet or cradle.

☐ Check to make sure that spaces between spindles are no larger than 2⅜ inches (60 mm).

☐ Check screws and bolts periodically to see if they are tight.

☐ If the product has legs that fold for storage, make sure that effective locks are provided to ensure that the legs do not accidentally fold while in use.

☐ Mattresses and padding should fit snugly and be firm and smooth. Never use pillows.

☐ Decorative bows and ribbons should be trimmed short and stitched securely to prevent strangulation.

☐ Swinging cradles should have a way to keep them from swinging once a baby is asleep.

Baby Crib: After some dusty digging in my parents' basement, I found my old baby crib. It was an adorable soft cream color with stenciled pale green teddy bears on the headboard. But after setting it up, I got a sinking feeling that what passed for state-of-the-art years ago wouldn't be safe or sturdy enough for my baby.

The CPSC says the best investment you can make for your daughter is a crib that meets all of its standards. This is important because, according to the CPSC, cribs account for more infant deaths than any other nursery item.

If you're buying a new full-size crib, the CPSC recommends you follow these guidelines:

☐ Corner posts should not extend more than ¹⁄₁₆ inch (1½ mm) above the top of the end panel. Corner posts can be catchpoints for clothing or items placed around a child's neck.

☐ Mattress support hangers should be secured by bolts or closed hooks. All crib hardware should be securely tightened and checked frequently.

☐ Bumper pads, if used, should (a) fit around the entire crib, (b) tie or snap into place, and (c) have straps or ties at least in each corner, in the middle of each long side, and on both the top and the bottom edges. To prevent your daughter from becoming entangled in the ties, trim off excess length after tying. Use the bumpers until your daughter can pull up to a

CRIB TOYS

Today's crib toys are so colorful and decorative that it's hard to resist the urge to buy them all! But a crowded crib can be an unsafe place for your baby to sleep. To stay on the safe side, always remove all toys, including stuffed animals, from the crib when the baby is present. Also, be sure to follow these guidelines from the CPSC when using baby gyms or mobiles in the crib:

• Make sure that crib gyms are installed securely at both ends so they cannot be pulled down into the crib.

• Remove crib gyms and mobiles when your daughter is five months old or begins to push up on her hands and knees.

• Mobiles and any other toys hanging over a crib or playpen should be out of your daughter's reach.

• Do not use crib toys with catch points that can hook clothing.

standing position, then remove them so that she will not use them to try to climb out of the crib.

☐ Remove and destroy all plastic wrapping materials. Never use plastic bags as mattress covers. The plastic film may cling to a baby's face and cause suffocation.

If you have a used crib, be extra careful about safety features. Although you might love to have that antique cradle or your sister's hand-me-down, keep in mind that the majority of cribs involved in fatal incidents were previously owned or used. Parents and caregivers reported obtaining these used cribs as "hand-me-downs" gifts from friends and relatives or by purchasing them at yard sales, flea markets, and used furniture stores. So, if you're using a hand-me-down crib, double check for these safety factors:

☐ Use a crib that meets federal safety regulations and industry voluntary standards and make sure it has a tight fitting mattress. (Check the labeling on these products to make sure they meet safety requirements.)

☐ Replace any missing parts, such as screws, bolts, or mattress support hangers before placing your daughter in it. Make sure all screws or bolts are securely tightened. Any screw inserted into a wood component that cannot be tightened securely should be replaced by one that fits. On cribs where the mattress support is suspended by hangers attached to hooks on the end panels, check frequently to be sure they have not become disconnected. Never use a crib with broken or missing parts.

☐ Use a mattress that fits snugly. If you can fit more than two fingers between the edge of the mattress and crib side, the mattress is too small. An infant can suffocate if her head or body becomes wedged between the mattress and the crib sides.

☐ Avoid older cribs with headboard and footboard designs that may allow an infant's head to become caught in the openings between the corner post and the top rail, or in other openings in the top edge of the headboard structure. These openings may lead to strangulation.

☐ Corner posts should be less than ¹⁄₁₆ inches high (1½ mm) unless the crib has a canopy. Do not use a crib with decorative knobs on corner posts. If you already have a crib with such knobs, they should be unscrewed or sawed off flush with the headboard or footboard. Sand off splinters and sharp corners.

☐ Never use a crib with loose or missing slats. Be sure that all slats are securely fastened in place and the space between slats is no more than 2⅜ inches (60 mm) to avoid head entrapment/strangulation.

☐ If you paint or refinish the crib, use only high-quality household lead-free enamel paint and let it dry thoroughly so there are no residual fumes. Check the label on the paint can to make sure the manufacturer does not recommend against using the paint on items such as cribs.

Insider Decorating Ideas for Girls Only

As my little family grew, we moved from an apartment to a small house to a larger house. In each home I set up another nursery. It was always so much fun imagining a new infant in the room and selecting just the right color scheme, bedding, changing table, and toys.

Since I'm no designing expert, I was curious to know what the professionals say about decorating a baby girl's nursery, so I contacted interior designer Mark Langos of Mark Langos Interior Design in Los Angeles, California. He is also the merchandising and design producer for *Area*, a home makeover show on Style network. Langos has just recently finished creating a nursery for his own infant daughter, which was featured in *Child* magazine. My nurseries never looked quite like the ones in magazines, so I asked Langos to tell us how he approached the task.

"Rather than choosing any specific theme, like a cartoon character or nursery rhyme," says Langos, "I chose to use color as the theme. I painted the walls and the ceiling a soft shade of pink, and then painted all the trim in the room a glossy white. I tend to like muted, washed-out colors that contain a lot of white and convey a feeling of peace and tranquillity. I felt the pink would have a calming and soothing effect on the baby."

Although Langos thinks that baby girl rooms look great in pink, yellow, or green, he says you can use any color, as long as it's not too bold. "The bolder colors energize children," he offers. "I wanted the nursery to be a place for quiet sleep." And before committing to a color, Langos suggests you experiment a bit. "Buy a quart of the color you like," he says, "and paint a 2×2-foot square patch on the wall. Examine that color in morning, noon, and nighttime light. You'll be surprised how much the color changes through the course of the day."

Once you've picked out your color scheme, it's time to choose the furniture and accessories. "Everything else we brought into the space (such as the crib, dresser, bookcase, shag rug, and toy chest) stuck to a very strict color regime of white," says Langos. "This allowed for a clean, calming backdrop. Limiting the furniture and accessories to the color white allowed us to mix a variety of different styles with color as the cohesive element. Our daughter's room has a great mix of both traditional and contemporary styles, which I think gives it a sophisticated, modern feeling. I know our daughter will easily grow into a little girl in this space, as we add color and vibrancy with different colors in pillows, rugs, or other accessories as she grows."

Speaking of "as she grows," keep in mind that your baby girl will grow. "When setting up your nursery," says Langos, "it's really important to remember that this baby is not going to be a baby forever and you don't have to buy all furniture and accessories in baby-supply stores. Too many parents invest a lot of time and money on an infant nursery that doesn't work for their three-year-old at all and needs to be completely redone by the time the child goes to school." For example, Langos chose an armoire that he now uses to hang his daughter's clothes and store her blankets. "But," he says, "I can imagine that as she grows older, this will be a good place for her computer and the drawers will then hold toys and art supplies. It's a flexible piece of furniture that can change as she grows."

Langos thinks it is also important to remember that you will also be spending a lot of time in this room (especially in the middle of the night while rocking your hungry or fussy girl back to sleep). So carve out a space for you, too. "An important piece of furniture in our baby's room is a really comfortable chair. We bought a glider/rocker that has a white, washable slipcover. This is so practical because we can throw the slipcover into the wash with some bleach to clean up all the baby slips and spit-ups."

So there you have it—straight from the designer's mouth. Go for soft colors with accessories and furniture that will grow with your daughter.

Baby Girl Toys

A newborn doesn't need many toys, especially the candy-colored stuffed animals they are likely to accumulate as gifts. In fact, it's safer to keep an infant's crib and play area free of toys.

But when you do buy toys for your baby girl, look them over carefully. All toys should have smooth edges and be nontoxic, nonbreakable, and washable. Never give a baby a toy smaller than 1⅝ inches across that can be swallowed (check all parts that may fall off and become a choking hazard). Cut off any ribbons and strings, and check all toys occasionally to be sure they are in good repair.

IT'S ALL IN THE BRAIN

Even before birth, there are differences between the male and female brain. The brain is 10 percent smaller in mass in girls than in boys, but the girl's corpus callosum (which connects the two hemispheres of the brain and helps coordinate the activities of the left and right hemisphere) is larger. The female brain produces more serotonin—a quieting agent, which may explain why the female fetus does not seem to be as active as the male.

TOYS FOR BABY GIRLS

Here is a list of toys that are worth considering for your baby girl:

- **Mobile:** A wind-up or electric mobile visible from the crib can give your daughter something interesting to look at while she's lying on her back. Many mobiles also play music. Be sure the mobile is securely fastened, out of her reach, and not hanging directly over the crib (just in case it falls). Crib mobiles should be removed by the time your daughter is able to get on her hands and knees, usually when she is about five or six months old. A mobile visible from the changing table can also help keep her amused during diaper changes.

- **Rattle:** Once your daughter can grasp something, she'll love rattles, especially if they have parts that spin or otherwise move. But buy your rattles with caution: Avoid those with ball-shaped ends. Check for small ends that could extend into the back of her mouth. Take rattles and other small objects out of the crib or playpen when she sleeps. And remember that, like pacifiers, rattles should never be fastened to a cord around your daughter's neck.

- **Padded play mats** placed on the floor, often with segments that crinkle or squeak, are fun for babies who cannot yet crawl.

- **Floor gyms** provide things for girls to grab and bat while they lie on their backs on the floor.

INDOOR SWING

Colleen loved her indoor swing. It was the one place I could put her down knowing I would have at least ten minutes of peace to wash some dishes (or my face!) and throw in a load of laundry while she happily swung back and forth, lulled by the rhythmic motion. I tell all my friends that this is a "must-have" piece of baby equipment.

Baby swings are semi-reclining seats that hang on rigid arms from a four-legged frame. Both electric and wind-up versions are available. Babies differ widely in their reaction to swings, so it's best to try them out before buying one, especially because they take up a lot of floor space.

If you do decide to buy a swing, check it carefully for safety. The base should have non-skid, sturdy legs. It must also have a seat belt and crotch restraint to hold your daughter's squirmy body in place. I prefer the battery-operated over the wind-up version because it can be reset without making a noise that might wake the baby. An adjustable seat is also a plus so you can recline it for your newborn and raise it as her neck gets stronger.

For Girls on the Go

It won't be long before you and your daughter are out and about. There are a few pieces of equipment you might want to have in the house before your baby girl arrives to make travel safe and easy. These include a diaper bag, front carrier, car seat, carrier seat, and stroller.

DIAPER BAG

Every time you leave home with your daughter, your diaper bag will go with you. Look for one that will hold up for the long haul. It should be washable and contain an insulated compartment for keeping bottles warm or cool. It should have various compartments for organizing the many baby items you'll need to find quickly while traveling (pacifier, baby wipes, rattle, bottles, diapers, ointment, burp cloth, and on and on). You should also consider buying the bag in a design and color (other than pastel baby prints) that both Mom and Dad will feel comfortable carrying.

FRONT CARRIER

You'll quickly find that newborn babies love to be held close to your heart. You'll also soon discover that doing this all day long makes it difficult to do anything else! That's why so many new parents love their baby carriers. Front carriers are best for newborns because they need the extra head support. You'll notice that the front carriers come in many different designs and shapes: Some look like a sling that hold the baby in a prone position; others are more sacklike and hold her upright against your chest. Either way, your daughter is kept warm, cozy, and near your body. As your daughter grows and gains weight, you'll probably want to switch to a back carrier, which puts less strain on your own back and gives her more opportunity to look around.

STROLLERS

Strollers these days are very portable and lightweight, but some don't hold up well when little girls begin to wiggle and turn. When shopping, look for a sturdy stroller that can hold its ground and won't tip over. Also look for one that has a sunshade and front wheels that pivot. It's also nice to have a model that reclines for comfortable napping.

Here are some tips for choosing a stroller:

☐ If you plan to use a stroller before your daughter can sit up, make sure the stroller fully reclines. With adult supervision, such a stroller can double as a portable bed for use indoors or in the park. Just make sure your baby daughter lies on her back and is belted in. The safest belt design is a T-buckle: a crotch strap and waist belt that connect together.

☐ Umbrella strollers—lightweight cloth slings with thin metal frames that fold like an accordion—do not provide enough support for newborns and usually don't recline. But they can be fine for short jaunts with a toddler.

☐ Make sure your stroller has a canopy to block the sun, preferably with a plastic window so you can see your daughter. (You won't need the window if your stroller handle reverses so your baby girl can face you while you push.)

☐ Check carefully for weight, ease of steering, and ease of folding. Weight it down with twenty or twenty-five pounds and then push it around the store. Try pushing with one hand—you should still be able to steer the stroller in a straight line. Try folding and unfolding it.

☐ For stability, the wheel base should be wide and the seat low in the frame. The stroller should resist tipping backward when you press down lightly on the handles.

☐ A roomy underseat bin can save your shoulders and back from the strain of carrying heavy bags.

Strolling with Two: Strollers for two come either in tandem style, where one child sits behind the other, or side by side. Not all side-by-sides can fit comfortably through a standard doorway, so check before you buy. Tandems are generally easier to maneuver, especially if you have riders of unequal weight—an infant and a toddler—rather than twins. They're also more compact when folded. But side-by-side transports allow both users to recline more comfortably at the same time. And being side by side may be more fun for them.

Jogging Strollers: These carriages, also called sports or running strollers, are designed to be pushed as the adult runs or jogs. They are elongated and have three large wheels—one in front and two in back—which make them easier to roll than regular strollers. They're also higher priced—starting at about $150—and too big for indoor use. If you're already a confirmed runner or brisk exercise walker, such a stroller may make sense. If you don't have a steady track record with exercise, they may be a waste.

In either case, go slow on getting a jogging stroller. Because of the shaking that comes with higher speed, it's best not to run or jog while pushing a baby until the child is about one year old. Even then, look for routes that are smooth underfoot.

CAR SEAT

By law, all children under age five must be strapped into a car seat when riding in a vehicle. This is so important that most hospitals will not release a baby until they are assured the parent has a car seat in the vehicle that will be taking the baby home. That's why you should make this purchase before you deliver your child.

Because your daughter will use this car seat for several years, it's worth the time to do some comparison shopping. Here are some basics to help you make the right choice:

Car seats are made in two basic styles:

1. **Infant seat:** This is designed for children under twenty pounds and faces toward the back of the car.

2. **Infant-toddler seat:** This can be used by both infants and older children up to forty pounds. It faces backward for infant use and is turned around to face front when the baby reaches twenty pounds.

When you are comparing car seats look for:

☐   **Price.** They run from around $50 to $200. Somewhere in the middle of the range is probably the best buy.

☐ **Easy installation.** If you can't install the seat correctly every time you put it in the car, it won't protect your daughter properly. Unfortunately, some seats make you jump through hoops to get it in place correctly. Make sure you feel comfortable with the installation process before you buy.

☐ **Seat belt adjustments.** Check out how the seat belt from the vehicle gets attached to the car seat. Some are easy; others require an engineering degree.

☐ **Washability.** If this is your first baby, you have no idea how messy the car seat can become. All kinds of dirt, food, drink, and vomited substances will find their way onto this new seat. Buy one with removable and washable pad covers.

☐ **Comfort.** Babies spend a lot of time in these seats. Find one that looks comfortable to sit in. Look for cloth padding (vinyl seats get very hot and can burn a baby's skin), along with head and back support. Also look for one that is high enough to let your daughter see out the window.

☐ **Safety.** Look for a label attached to the car seat saying that it meets or exceeds Motor Vehicle Safety Standards (sometimes abbreviated as FMVSS 213). Any other kind of seat should never be used in a car.

CARRIER SEAT

This little reclining chair can come in very handy. It lets your daughter sit up and watch you while you work around the

STAY AWAY FROM THESE!

- Pillows, quilts, sheepskins, soft mattresses, or any other kind of soft bedding. Also, stuffed animals or other soft toys should be kept out of the crib or bassinet. Keeping your daughter's sleeping area free of such objects appears to lower the risk of Sudden Infant Death Syndrome (SIDS) which, according to the American SIDS Institute at www.sids.org, is the sudden death of an infant under one year of age which remains unexplained after a thorough case investigation.

- Tub seats. These are intended for use in a bathtub by babies old enough to sit up. But experts advise against using them: They may tempt a parent to leave the baby alone in the tub, which can be extremely dangerous, and potentially fatal.

- Talc (baby) powder. If inhaled, it can irritate the lungs.

- Latex balloons. Uninflated or broken, they pose a choking hazard.

house and it holds her in a good position for feeding. Unfortunately, this kind of seat can cause severe injury to an infant if it should fall, especially off a high table. Your little ballerina will soon be pirouetting and throwing her weight around, so look for an infant seat with a nonskid, wide bottom that will discourage tipping. And never leave your daughter alone in an infant seat.

To safely use a carrier seat, follow these safety tips:

☐ The carrier should have a wide, sturdy base for stability.

☐ Stay within arm's reach of your daughter when the carrier seat is on tables, counters, or other furniture. Never turn your back. Carrier seats slide more easily on slippery surfaces, such as glass tabletops.

☐ If the carrier seat does not already have nonskid feet, attach rough-surfaced adhesive strips to the underside.

☐ Always use the carrier's safety belts and keep them snug.

☐ If the carrier seat contains wire supporting devices that snap on the back, check for security. These can pop out, causing the carrier seat to collapse.

☐ Never place a carrier seat on soft surfaces such as beds or sofas. The carrier seat may tip over and your daughter may strangle or suffocate.

☐ Remember that a carrier seat does not always double as an infant car seat, and should never be used in an automobile unless it is labeled for that purpose.

The End of B.B.

Planning for a little girl is such fun. Tracking her female growth through your pregnancy, choosing just the right name, finding a good doctor, and then shopping for the must-have newborn items will fill your B.B. (before baby) time with dreams of sugar and spice and everything nice. Then before you know it, you'll have your little girl in your arms. That's when the real fun begins!

MY BABY GIRL

"The best things about having a daughter are: tea parties, having a shopping buddy, planning their wedding, and having someone who is a reflection of my own childhood."

—Lisa Cannizzo, mother of three daughters

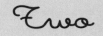

Your Infant Daughter:

From Birth Through Three Months

What a precious treasure your baby girl is! Like an adored princess, she has entered your world to be admired and cared for. If you gaze too long into her innocent eyes, she will steal your heart and make you her loving servant. With gratitude and devotion you will answer her every cry and gladly fill all her demands. This soft and sweet bundle of love now rules your home, sometimes as a screaming tyrant and other times as an affectionate cherub.

During these first three months you are in training to learn her likes and dislikes, her moods and personality, her needs and desires. It can be an unnerving period. But her first smile, adorable coos, and loving stare will make it all worthwhile.

You and your daughter are in this together and will surely finish up the first three months bound by mutual love and devotion.

Welcome to the World, Baby Girl!

My daughter, Colleen, was my third child—and my first daughter. Her beauty, as rumpled as it was at birth, took my breath away. She was an answer to prayer—and an angel sent from God. But I still held her with hesitation. She seemed so fragile and a bit "unfinished." Your daughter, too, may not look quite like the baby you've been dreaming of. Instead, she'll look like an infant who has left a watery womb and been squished through a rather small vaginal opening. Don't be surprised or upset if your daughter has any of the following less-than-attractive features, all of which are temporary:

- The cheesy substance that coats a baby's skin to protect it from the amniotic fluid (called vernix caseosa) may still be covering parts of her body.

- After a vaginal birth, the head may appear elongated, almost cone-shaped, because it was compressed coming through the birth canal. This will round out within two weeks.

- Fine, downy hair (called lanugo) may cover the shoulders, back, forehead, and temples. This will usually be gone by the end of the first week. It will last longer on a premature infant.

- Swollen genitals are common. Due to maternal hormones, your baby girl's breasts may also be enlarged. This will disappear in a week to ten days.

■ Puffy eyes are usually caused by the eye drops given to infants immediately after birth to prevent infection.

Despite all these less-than-lovely features, there's no doubt your daughter will look absolutely beautiful to you and your partner. After all the time and work you've put into bringing her into the world, you can see how truly miraculous this tiny human being really is.

Baby's First Medical Exam

If your daughter is born in a hospital, her first screaming wail as she enters the world and announces her arrival will be a test of her overall health. The details vary from hospital to hospital, but the basics of what happens after that remain the same.

THE APGAR EVALUATION

One minute after her birth, your daughter will take her first test, called an *Apgar evaluation*. This rating system is named after its originator, Dr. Virginia Apgar, and is used to evaluate how well she adapts to the outside world. Dr. Apgar's name is now used as an acronym for five areas of evaluation:

A: appearance (especially skin color)

P: pulse rate (number of heartbeats per minute)

G: grimace (a baby's response to annoying stimulation, such as a tap or a finger flick to the body)

A: activity (muscle tone is tested through observation and by flexing and feeling the tension in the baby's arms and legs)

R: respiration (how well the baby can breathe and cry on her own)

Each of these factors is rated on a scale of 0 to 2, with 2 being the most desirable, making for a perfect score of 10. A score of 7 or more indicates the baby is in good condition. A score under 7 indicates the baby is in some kind of distress and needs careful observation or medical attention. The test is repeated five minutes later. A low score is not cause for panic—most babies with low scores turn out to be normal and healthy.

ROUTINE NEWBORN CARE

In between Apgar evaluations, your daughter will receive routine newborn care. The doctor or nurse draws a tube of blood from the placental umbilical cord, which is used to identify the baby's blood type and Rh group and may be used for umbilical cord blood banking. At that point, the medical staff or midwife generally will:

- Clear her nasal passages with a bulb syringe so she can breathe easily.

- Weigh your daughter, measure her length and head circumference, take her temperature, and estimate her gestational age.

- Put antibiotic ointment or drops in her eyes to prevent infection.

■ Take her footprints or palm print for identification, and give both baby and her mom ID bracelets or anklets. The nurse will check these IDs each time the child is brought to you after being out of your sight. (Although some hospitals are now using new blood typing techniques for this identification, the foot- and fingerprinting routine is still common.)

■ Dry her, wrap her in a blanket, put a tiny knitted cap on her head, and perhaps place her in a warmed bassinet (or on the mother's chest), to prevent heat loss. (Newborns cannot regulate their temperatures as well as adults.)

The order in which these things get done vary. If your daughter is born in a hospital, these tasks may be done right in the delivery room or in the nursery. Either way, you will probably be given one more chance to hold your daughter before you are moved to the recovery room and she heads to the nursery. Savor and enjoy this moment. It is one you will want to remember forever.

NEWBORN SCREENING TEST (NBU)

With these tests behind her, your daughter will have some time to rest and adjust to her world before the next test begins. Within the first twenty-four to forty-eight hours of her life, she will be given the newborn screening test (NBU)—also called the heel-stick test—to screen for various diseases or conditions, such as phenylketonuria (PKU) and congenital hypothyroidism (which strikes girls twice as often as boys), for which early treatment can prevent physical and developmental delays, or even death. The test is performed by pricking your daughter's heel and putting a few drops of blood on a special filter paper. The paper is allowed to dry and then sent to the newborn screening laboratory where several different tests will be performed.

All states require a newborn screening test, but each state screens for different disorders. Although the NBU is capable of screening for more than fifty disorders, most states screen for less than eight. You can find out which tests your state screens for from Save Babies Through Screening Foundation on the website at www.savebabies.org. This site will also tell you how to send a blood sample to a private lab for a complete screening if you choose.

Mealtime: Bottle or Breast?

All three of my children were breast-fed, yet each experience was entirely different. The decision to breast- or bottle-feed depends on so many factors that no one can tell you what's right or wrong for you. Other mothers can share their experiences and offer some advice, but in the end, you are the only person who can know what is best for you and your daughter.

Breast-feeding has gained in popularity with today's generation of child-bearing-age women mostly because of the medical benefits it offers to the baby. It is known to strengthen her immune system and help prevent allergies, asthma, and SIDS. Breast milk also contains substances that help protect a baby from infections until her own immune system matures. It's also true that babies are less likely to have an allergic reaction to breast milk than to cow's milk.

And, of course, it is more readily available and cost-efficient than formula.

But many new moms choose to bottle-feed for reasons that are equally important. They may be on medications that could pass through the breast milk and have negative effects on the baby. They may be working and need the convenience of bottle-feeding for the baby's care-givers. They may have a chronic infection such as HIV that could pass to the baby through breast milk. They may have had breast surgery, making breast-feeding difficult. Or they have the best reason of all: They simply don't want to.

Both bottle and breast-fed babies grow to be healthy, well-adjusted human beings. Don't feel righteous or guilty about whichever method you use. Just do whichever is best for you, and enjoy every moment you hold your daughter in your arms and provide her with both physical and emotional nourishment.

BOTTLE-FEEDING

The joy of bottle-feeding is that it allows everyone to have a turn at feeding the new baby—your partner, your daughter's older siblings, your parents, and your in-laws can all chip in and discover the wonderful feeling of closeness that comes from holding and nourishing a newborn. Your daughter will probably take to the bottle easily; bottle nipples are easier for a newborn to grasp onto than the breast. But if your daughter doesn't seem interested in eating right away, don't push. For the first few days, she probably won't be very hungry as she recovers from delivery and adjusts to her new surroundings. Soon, however, her appetite will pick up.

Once you make the decision to bottle-feed, you'll face the decision of which kind of formula to use. (Cow's milk straight from the dairy case in your store does not have the nutrients a baby needs in the first year.) Pediatricians recommend a cow's milk–based formula for most babies, and then suggest switching to a soy-based formula if any problems occur. Soy formulas are recommended for infants with a family history of milk allergies.

After deciding between cow's milk and soy-based, you can purchase formula in three different forms: ready-to-use, liquid concentrate, and powder. Obviously, the ready-to-use is the easiest form, but it also the most expensive. If you choose concentrate or powder, be sure to follow the mixing and storage instructions to the letter. Diluting with too much or too little water can harm your daughter. Make sure the filled bottles are refrigerated until it is time to use them. When traveling, put them in thermal bags, which keep them cold. Once you have opened a can of prepared formula or put formula into bottles, use it within forty-eight hours.

Formula should be "served" at room temperature—not warm and certainly not hot. Getting the formula to room temperature is quite an art and very different from the way your mother warmed your bottles. Do not put a bottle in boiling water on the stovetop and do not heat it in the microwave. These methods overheat the food and destroy nutrients. The microwave is especially dangerous. Because it heats from the inner core out, it is possible for some of the liquid to be scalding hot, and you won't know it until your daughter drinks it. Shaking the bottle does not reduce the danger from one of these hot spots. Instead, cold or even frozen formula (and stored breast milk, too) should be held under warm running water until it becomes room temperature. Or, you can use a commercial bottle warmer.

Most pediatricians recommend that all baby bottles be sterilized before use until the infant is three months old. You can do this by using a bottle sterilizer found at any baby-supply store. Or, you can simply use the dishwasher. But be sure to place plastic items on the top shelf and use a dishwasher-safe container to hold small items such as nipples and rings to keep them from getting caught up in the motor. You can also sterilize bottles by boiling them in a large pot of water on top of the stove for five minutes. After sterilizing, store bottles in the refrigerator to keep them bacteria-free.

Once you have all your equipment in hand, it's time to feed your daughter. No matter what your well-meaning relatives tell you, feed your newborn on demand. Although she probably won't need a feeding as often as breast-fed babies (because formula is more filling), she will still let you know when she is hungry, and you should answer the call. Start with a four-ounce bottle and let your daughter decide when she's had enough—don't try to cajole her into finishing it all if she is clearly full. If you have formula left over, throw it away; it is a breeding ground for bacteria once the baby has sucked from the bottle.

BREAST-FEEDING

Breast-feeding is the most natural thing in the world—but that doesn't mean it comes naturally. Many new mothers have a bit of trouble at first getting their babies to successfully nurse at the breast. So, if this is what you want to do, don't get frustrated and give up too quickly. You and your daughter need time and patience to get to know each other and find a system that works best for both of you. The following tips will help you get a good start.

Getting Started: If this is your first time breast-feeding, you will naturally feel uncertain about exactly how this is supposed to work. Complicating that feeling of confusion is the fact that your daughter may not know what to do either. Some babies latch on like old pros while others root around, looking for food. If your daughter is having trouble, give her some help. You can activate the rooting reflex by gently stroking her cheek with your finger or your nipple. This will cause your daughter to turn toward your breast.

Now she has to latch on to your nipple and that's not always easy. You can help out by making sure her mouth encircles the entire nipple area, called the areola, not just the nipple itself. If her mouth encircles the nipple only, you both will be uncomfortable. This can cause your nipples to become sore or even crack, and your daughter may not get all the milk she needs. Place your nipple in the center of her mouth, with the areola entirely within her lips. Make sure that your breast does not cover her nose and interfere with breathing.

When you begin nursing, it's best to start slowly. Many newborns have very little appetite for the first few days of life and your breasts need to ease into the process gradually. At first, allow your daughter about five minutes on each breast. Over the course of a few days, and depending on your daughter's appetite, you can build up to ten minutes per breast and then to fifteen. You should also start nursing on the opposite breast at each feeding. This will keep milk being produced evenly by both breasts. To break the baby's suction when you're ready to switch breasts, simply place your finger into her mouth, between the nipple and her mouth. And be sure to burp your daughter before switching to the other breast and after the feeding is over. (See page 56 for a few tips on burp-ing.)

For the first few days, your daughter won't be getting much ac-tual milk. Your breasts will produce a yellowish liquid called colostrums that is rich in antibodies and protective cells from your bloodstream. These substances help your newborn fight off infec-tions until her own immune system matures. After about five days, the colostrums will diminish and milk will take over.

How Often to Breast-feed: Your daughter knows how often she should be fed. She will let you know—loud and clear. Some babies are voracious eaters and others are quite finicky. In general, breast-fed babies eat more than formula-fed babies because breast milk is less filling than formula. But your daughter will determine her own schedule and let you know when she's hungry by fussing, making sucking noises, and by crying.

For the first week or so, your daughter will probably need to nurse quite often because her stomach can't hold enough to keep her satisfied for long periods. Every hour is not uncommon. Be-cause nursing can take anywhere from ten to thirty minutes, a hun-gry infant can take up most of your day.

After a few days, your daughter will have the hang of how to suckle just as her appetite kicks in. The regular sucking motions in her face and the gulping sounds will tell you that she is feeding well. You can't measure precisely how much your daughter is drinking, but it's comforting to know that your milk supply is de-termined by how much the baby sucks. If she needs more milk, her increased sucking will prompt your body to produce more milk.

This keeps the amount of milk you have and your daughter's needs in sync.

Keep your eyes open for signs that your daughter is getting enough nutrition. She should be wetting her diaper from five to eight times a day during the first few days and from six to eight times a day afterwards. And she should be gaining weight at a rate that satisfies her doctor. When this is the case, you can feel satisfied that she is getting all the nourishment she needs.

Hand-Expressing Breast Milk: Most nursing mothers find that at some point they need to hand-express their milk. I found that when my breasts were overloaded with milk, expressing eased the pain. I also expressed milk into baby bottles to store for later use when a babysitter or my husband would be feeding the baby. For either need, I found expressing milk to be an easy process.

Always wash your hands before you begin to express milk. Then, to express by hand, hold a clean container under your breast and place one hand around your breast with the thumb on top. Gently squeeze in a rhythmic fashion, pulling the thumb toward the areola. It's easiest to master this technique when your breasts are full.

You can also express your milk with a manual or electric breast pump. A pump is more efficient if you need to express bottles of milk on a regular basis. Carefully follow the manufacturer's instructions and ask for help from a more experienced friend. Then wash and sterilize the pump immediately after each use, or as soon as possible.

Storing Breast Milk: Be very careful about how you store your breast milk. It must always be placed immediately in the refrigerator or freezer. (If you're away from home, store it in an insulated cooler.) It should be used within twenty-four hours if refrigerated, or three months if frozen. If the milk will be stored for a while, put a label on the bottle and date it. If it's to be frozen, don't use a glass bottle or fill the container completely. Milk expands as it freezes. Refrigerated or frozen breast milk may look different in the bottle because the fat separates from the liquid. It's still good. Just warm the bottle under hot running water or place it in a bowl of hot water. Do not leave it out at room temperature. Also, don't heat the milk in a microwave or on the stovetop. The immune properties of breast milk are heat sensitive and the uneven heating of a microwave risks scalding the baby. Never refreeze partially used or thawed milk.

Using Breast and Bottle Milk: There may be times when you don't have the time or interest to express milk, and instead choose to use formula bottle-feeding. Many new moms alternate between the two. If you decide to do this, you'll need to be careful not to bottle-feed more often than you breast-feed. The bottle's nipple is easier for your daughter to suck than your breast, so sucking from a bottle can make her lazy about sucking from the breast. Also, if you offer formula in a bottle too often, your breasts will reduce the amount of milk they produce.

Easing Discomfort: Even with the best intentions and care, sometimes breast-feeding causes breast discomfort and even pain. A common problem is called engorgement. This happens if your breasts are not emptied during each feeding, and it can be very painful. My breasts quickly became engorged after the birth of my daughter and I worried that I had made a mistake in choosing to breast-feed. Fortunately, an understanding nurse taught me two very helpful methods of reducing the pain of engorgement: 1) express milk between feedings to reduce the pressure, and 2) apply warm compresses immediately before feedings to encourage the milk to flow freely. What a relief!

Nursing may make your nipples sore or even cracked until they toughen up. To relieve this discomfort, expose your nipples to the air as much as possible. Pamper them with ultrapurified, medical-grade lanolin, A&D ointment, or vitamin E (squeezed from capsules). Wash your nipples with water only; do not use soaps or remoistened towelettes. After each feeding, express some milk and massage it onto your nipples. Vary your nursing position so that a different part of the nipple will be compressed at each feeding. Hand-express some milk before feeding so that the nipple is easier for your daughter to grasp. This pain should last only for about one week. If it continues, talk to your doctor.

Calling for Help: If you have any trouble, questions, or concerns about breast-feeding, be sure to ask for help. Your doctor may assist you, or you might call in breast-feeding professionals. A lactation consultant at your local hospital, a woman's health center, or at the La Leche League can help you and your daughter adjust to each other. You can contact the La Leche League at 1-800-LALECHE or www.lalecheleague.org.

FEEDING AND BURPING TIPS

Here are some tips that will help you develop the art of burping and nighttime feedings.

Burping: For you and me, burping comes naturally, but not so for your daughter. Her gastrointestinal system isn't yet ready to do this work by itself and needs a little help from you. So allow time at every feeding to gently tap her on the back to nudge out a burp or two.

There are several positions you can choose for the burping routine. Try them all and pick the ones that feel most comfortable and do the job (but always remember to hold a cloth diaper or towel under the baby's mouth to catch the milk that often comes up with the burp):

1. While your daughter's head is still wobbly, it's easiest to burp her on your shoulder. Rest her head on your shoulder, use one arm to support her weight under the buttocks, and use the other hand to pat her on the back.

2. Sit your daughter on your lap, supporting her chest and head with one hand. Keeping her tilted slightly forward, and pat her back with your other hand.

3. Place your daughter, tummy down, across your thighs. Just slightly, lower her legs supporting her lower half so her head is higher than her chest. Gently pat her back or rub it in a circular motion.

Breast-fed babies generally burp less than bottle-fed babies because they take in less air. But you'll have to experiment with your daughter to determine her "burping personality." Some babies are gassier than others and burp often and with vigor; others give just a few soft burps. Either way, you should routinely burp your daughter, between switching breasts if nursing, or after every two

SCIENCE SAYS

Because infant girls are easier to handle, they often get less attention from their moms. That's the finding of a classic study of sex differences conducted by Howard Moss at the National Institutes of Mental Health. This study of thirty first-time moms found that at age three weeks, baby sons fussed more, cried more, and were more difficult to calm, while baby girls were more often alert, more responsive to efforts to calm them, and slept an average of one hour longer every twenty-four hours. This extra fussing by the boys caused their moms to hold them more, to move and stimulate them more, and in general give them more of their attention. The baby girls, who seemed more mature and less in need of help to become calm or to remain alert, received less holding, moving, and stimulation.

or three ounces of formula if bottle-feeding. Then, even if she has drifted off to sleep, be sure to burp her at the end of a feeding before putting her down to rest.

Nighttime Feedings: Unlike the rest of your household, your newborn doesn't know the difference between night and day. It's all the same to her and when she's hungry, she's hungry. So until your daughter's stomach is large enough to hold more milk—usually when she is about twelve pounds—she will not be able to sleep through the night without waking and crying for food. To establish a nighttime routine that encourages nighttime sleeping, make the night feedings a quiet, quick affair. Change the baby's diaper in a dimly lit room, feed, burp, and return her to her bed. No playing, bright lights, or loud talking. The time between feedings should gradually get longer and longer until finally your daughter is sleeping through the night by 12 to 16 weeks.

Getting Your Daughter to Sleep

The one thing most of us need in our life is a good night's sleep. You may be completely baffled to learn your infant daughter did not inherit this need. Darkness and daylight mean nothing to her. She will sleep and stay awake whenever she wants. And it will often seem that her desires are exactly the opposite of your own. While you may prefer to sleep at night, you'll soon learn that babies have other plans for the nighttime hours.

A BABY GIRL'S SLEEP SCHEDULE

At first, your newborn will sleep most of the day (about sixteen out of twenty-four hours) and wake about every three or four hours for a feeding. After about a week, she'll begin to spend more and more time awake and more time feeding. But it's still too early to set up any kind of sleep or feeding schedule. An infant's stomach is too small to hold enough food to last for long stretches between feedings.

From one to two months of age, infants spend more daytime hours awake, taking in the world around them. Still, most babies this age need at least 2 one-to-three-hour naps every day—one in the morning and one after lunch. If your daughter sleeps longer than three or four hours during daytime naps, wake her up so she will be sleepy at bedtime. At this age, many infants begin to skip at least one nighttime feeding. You can encourage a longer stretch between nighttime feedings by letting your daughter cry and fuss a bit before running to the rescue. Very often babies awake at night (as we all do) and just need a few minutes of fussing to settle back down and fall asleep again. Give your daughter a chance to learn how to self-soothe. You'll be glad you did when she is able to put herself back to sleep without your help over the next year.

At this time, you can emphasize the differences between night and day by keeping the baby's sleeping room dark at night and doing the necessary feeding and changing in a quick, quiet way. Don't talk, play, or turn on the lights. During the day, let the sunshine in, let the noise and bustle level stay higher, and play and talk with your daughter whenever she is awake. Unless your newborn is particularly sensitive to noise, it pays to keep daytime noise levels normal even when she is napping. That way she'll get used to snoozing through ringing phones and normal conversation.

By six weeks, babies tend to sleep longest in the evening, usually for three to five hours at a stretch, and this trend becomes stronger as the months pass. If you feed her at 10 or 11 P.M., you may even be able to sleep until dawn. At about three months, most bottle-fed babies no longer need feedings at night, even though they may enjoy them. Breast-fed babies usually reach that point a little later, perhaps at five or six months.

By three months, your daughter will be ready to have a more formal sleep schedule. You can begin to put her down at the same time every day for naps and bedtime. Remember to put her to sleep while she's still awake and not feeding. If you feed your daughter to sleep, she will need you to do it again and again every time she wakes in the middle of the night. Once she learns to associate feeding with sleeping, it will be hard to break the habit and she will want to suck in order to fall asleep every night. Throughout the night when she wakes naturally, she'll find she can't put herself back to sleep without feeding (or the pacifier!). This is also bad for her developing teeth. When the teeth begin to break through at about four months, bedtime feedings make cavities far more likely because the liquid pools around the teeth as the baby sleeps. So after feeding, wake your daughter, burp her, then put her down so she learns how to put herself to sleep without a feeding.

SHARING THE FAMILY BED

It's the middle of the night and your daughter is crying for a feeding. "Why not let her sleep in my bed so I don't have to keep getting up?" you wonder. There are many parents who strongly support the family bed and the emotional advantages they feel it gives to the whole family. On the other hand, there are many who see this arrangement as both an intrusion of privacy and a dangerous situation for the child.

In my case, I did not bring my baby daughter to my bed because my three-year-old son was still there! I had let him move in as an infant and he had no intention of moving out to make room for his little sister. The family bed did not work well for me!

The final decision on whether or not to bring your daughter into your bed is entirely up to you. If you decide to make room for a squiggly infant (even if it's just for the feeding) keep these safety tips in mind:

WHEN YOU'RE SERIOUSLY SLEEPY

Despite all the kidding, long-term sleep deprivation for parents or other caretakers can be very unpleasant. It can also be dangerous, leading to accidents at home and in the car, marital tension, and even child abuse when overtired parents lash out at a crying child. The effects of going without sleep tend to be cumulative, building up over months. Take them seriously. Especially in those first few weeks, remember the number-one rule of parent preservation: Sleep when the baby sleeps. Or, if you can't sleep, at least lie down and rest.

☐ Remove all pillows and comforters. Your daughter can't push them out of the way if they get pulled over her face while you sleep. Also do not bring a baby into your bed if you sleep on a waterbed, feather bed, or sheepskin. They, too, can cause suffocation.

☐ Do not bring your daughter into your bed if you are under the influence of alcohol, medications, or other drugs. You will not hear her cry if you roll over on her and suffocate her. (Sadly, it has happened.)

☐ Be sure your daughter can easily sleep on her back to avoid SIDS.

☐ Don't over-bundle your daughter; she will have your body heat as well as her own. Overheating is one suspected cause of SIDS.

☐ Put your daughter in the middle of the bed so she can't roll off. (Even newborns work their way across the bed as your own body shifts positions during the night.)

Crying Babies

As precious and adorable as your new baby girl may be, you'll soon discover that she has a mighty set of lungs that can shatter the household calm without warning, day or night. The first cry after birth fills your newborn's lungs with air and expels any fluid. By two to three weeks of age, infants typically start to develop a type of fussy crying. Most babies have a fussy spell between 6 and 10 P.M. (just when you are apt to feel most frazzled) and sometimes it worsens as the evening goes on. After that, babies cry for many reasons: they are tired, hungry, bored, wet, uncomfortable—or for no apparent reason at all.

Your instinct to go to your daughter when she cries is nature's way of making sure she learns that she is loved and cared for. So don't let well-meaning family and friends tell you that you'll spoil your daughter by picking her up when she cries. Charles Schaefer, Ph.D., a child psychologist and author of dozens of child-rearing books, says that when a parent responds quickly to a baby's cry in the first few weeks of life, the newborn feels nurtured. "For the first six months, it is unlikely you will spoil your daughter by swiftly responding to each cry or by surrendering to your impulse to cuddle and comfort," he assures us. "During this time many babies need a great deal of comforting to help ease the transition between intrauterine and independent life. Also, these babies do not have the ability to make the mental connection that enables older children to reason, 'If I cry, I'll get my own way.' Infant cries can, and should, be answered."

SOOTHING TECHNIQUES FOR YOUR CRYING BABY GIRL

Here are a few soothing techniques that Dr. Schaefer recommends for calming a crying baby:

Physical Contact: Pick up and cuddle your daughter as often as you like. Remember, for the first six months, you will not spoil her by giving her too much attention. In fact, babies whose cries are answered promptly in the first three months tend to cry less later on that those whose cries were often ignored. If your daughter calms when you carry her, but you can't carry her all day long and get anything else done, use an infant sling to keep her close to your body while you move around, getting on with your own activities.

Rhythmic Motion: Many babies stop crying when in motion. Rocking chairs, baby swings, carriage rides, and car rides are all modes of movement that calm many wailing babies.

Swaddling: Swaddling in a lightweight receiving blanket often restores a newborn's sense of comfort and closeness. That's why babies are routinely swaddled in hospital nurseries to reduce fearful crying. To swaddle at home, take one corner of a receiving blanket and fold it down six inches. Place the baby on the blanket with her head above the fold. Next, take one side of the blanket and draw it across her body. Fold the bottom section up over her feet, then fold the last section across her body. If she cries harder after swaddling, don't persist. Some babies find it too confining.

Noise: Run the vacuum cleaner near your daughter to provide a constant humming sound (don't feel you have to actually vacuum!). The static of an off radio channel, the hum of a laundry washer or dryer, or a tape recording of a waterfall, running shower, or heartbeat are all sounds parents have found will calm a fussy baby.

Comfort Sucking: Some babies have strong sucking needs unrelated to their desire for food. Their crying is often controlled by sucking on their fingers, fist, or a pacifier. (Most babies discontinue this extra sucking around age one.) If you choose to use a pacifier, it should be introduced in the first six to eight weeks (but wait until breast milk is well established after four to eight weeks if you're breast-feeding, to avoid "nipple confusion"). Use pacifiers made from only one piece of rubber; avoid those that can come apart. (Once your daughter decides on a certain type, it's

WHEN TO CALL THE DOCTOR

If your daughter seems overly irritable and cannot be soothed, or is difficult to rouse from sleep and seems uninterested in feeding, speak to your doctor. Chances are everything is fine, but it's worth getting medical guidance.

smart to buy a few extra you can use when one ends up on the floor or is chewed by the dog.) Don't coat the pacifier with sugary sweeteners. This habit can cause cavities later on. *Never tie the pacifier to a string that is then tied around your daughter's neck*—this could cause strangulation. Take the pacifier away from your daughter before bed or naps so she doesn't become dependent on it for going to sleep. Pacifiers can gradually be taken away between ages six to twelve months before she grows too dependent on it.

Singing: Even if you can't carry a tune, singing in a melodic and calm refrain may have magical soothing powers. Some researchers say that certain sounds and melodies, such as lullabies, can provide reassurance for babies by creating a sense of emotional security. So sing to your daughter often to help her build this association that will provide you with an always-available source of comfort.

Dealing with a fussy baby may be the most exhausting part of early parenting. It can leave you feeling helpless and like a failure, or frustrated and enraged, possibly even setting the stage for child abuse. If there's no help at hand and you feel at the end of your rope, it's better to put a crying baby in a safe place and leave the room, rather than risk shaking or otherwise hurting her.

It is far better to get some relief before the crying pushes you to the edge. If a spouse can't help, ask a relative to help out or hire someone for a few hours a day and get out of the house. Join a mothering center or parenting group. Oftentimes the support of other parents—or honest discussion and sympathy between you and your partner—is all you need to get through these tough weeks. Try to take advantage of those times when the baby is asleep and resting. And remember, as my mother told me time and time again, this too shall pass. (And she was right.)

Postpartum Disorders

In recent years, the often-ignored and misunderstood mood imbalance postpartum depression (PPD) has become a household word. As you recover from the birth of your daughter, you should be aware of the symptoms of postpartum depression, but also understand that there are varying degrees of this mood disorder and not all lead to murder.

POSTPARTUM BABY BLUES

What some call "postpartum blues" or "baby blues" is a mild form that the American College of Obstetricians and Gynecologists says affects about 70 to 85 percent of new moms. Within the first three days after giving birth, feelings of fatigue, nervousness, confusion, detachment from the baby, and anxiety accompanied by frequent bouts of crying set in. Most medical experts agree that these blues are caused by dramatic physiological changes that occur in hormonal levels after birth. (Levels of estrogen and progesterone drop as much as tenfold!) Social factors such as lack of family support and psychological factors such as marital tension can also play a role in causing and/or aggravating this mild form of PPD. Baby blues generally go away without any form of treatment within a week or two.

POSTPARTUM DEPRESSION

Postpartum depression (which affects about 10 percent of new mothers) is more intense and lasts longer than the blues. It can develop at almost any time up to one year after childbirth, but most often appears sometime between the second week and third month after birth. Typically, it can last anywhere from several weeks to several months.

Moderate PPD is apparently rooted in negative social and psychological factors. These tensions may include the daily stresses of parenting, feelings of isolation, a colicky infant, chronic lack of sleep, and marital tensions. It is best treated with professional help because it often responds well to a combination of antidepressant medication and cognitive therapy that teaches women to better cope with the stresses of parenthood.

If you have feelings of moderate PPD, you should not ignore them or let them go untreated. Dr. Schaefer says that if a few weeks go by and you are not yet feeling any enthusiasm about motherhood, or if you still aren't experiencing normal eating and sleeping patterns, you should call your physician or the support group (see "Warning Signs of Postpartum Depression" on page 69). In rare cases, the symptoms will persist and greatly increase in severity. This may indicate the onset of the most serious form of PPD, called postpartum psychosis.

POSTPARTUM PSYCHOSIS

Postpartum psychosis (PPP) affects only about 1 in 1,000 women and most often occurs during the first four weeks after delivery.

WARNING SIGNS OF POSTPARTUM DEPRESSION

The American College of Obstetricians and Gynecologists warns us that women with postpartum depression have feelings of being overwhelmed, are unable to cope with daily tasks, and feel guilty about not being a good enough mother. Other symptoms include:

deep sadness   intense anxiety
apathy   inability to sleep
lack of appetite   irrational behavior
crying spells   highly impaired concentration and
irritability   decision-making

Women with PPP are severely impaired and may have paranoia, mood shifts, or hallucinations and delusions that frequently focus on the infant's dying or being demonic. These hallucinations often command the woman to hurt herself or her baby. This condition requires immediate medical attention and, usually, hospitalization.

CARING FOR SYMPTOMS OF POSTPARTUM MOOD DISORDER

In the book *Raising Baby Right* Dr. Schaefer suggests that if you are feeling the symptoms listed in the box "Warning Signs of Postpartum Depression" you should follow these two steps:

1. Take care of yourself. Learn to recognize your overload factors and avoid them. If you feel you can't keep the house clean *and* take care of the baby, let the house go. If the visits of family and friends send you into a tizzy as you try to be a good host and cater to the needs of your newborn, take the phone off the hook and disconnect the doorbell. Get a sitter and make time to go for a walk, take a warm bath, and then a nap. Stay alert to the signs of depression and talk to your doctor if you start to feel them. Take care of yourself first and foremost. If you do this, you'll have the emotional and physical strength you need to take care of all your other responsibilities.

2. Seek support. Don't try to handle your negative feelings alone. These feelings do not mean you are a bad mother. They don't in any way indicate that you can't handle motherhood. They are very common feelings shared, to some degree, by approximately eight out of ten new mothers—the majority of whom turn out to be wonderful parents.

Talk to your spouse. He can't understand your feelings and actions unless you explain what's going on. His emotional support is very important to your ability to overcome your problem. Ask him for that help.

Talk to other mothers. Sharing your frustrations lessens their load, and hearing about similar experiences will take away some of the horror and mystery of this trying period.

Talk to your doctor. He or she can help you determine the level of your depression and decide on a treatment plan that will give you back your enthusiasm for parenthood.

Postpartum depression is very treatable, so you should get medical help promptly if you are depressed most of the time for two weeks or more.

Caring for Your Daughter in the Early Weeks

In the first three months, there's so much to think—and worry—about. Right from the start, you'll need to care for the health and hygiene of your daughter. Top on the list of things to do will be: caring for her umbilical cord stub, tending to the endless task of diapering (and diapering, and diapering), and, of course, bathing.

CARE OF THE UMBILICAL CORD

When the baby's umbilical cord is cut at the time of delivery, a small stump attached to the navel area remains. This umbilical-cord stump does not need exceptional care. Just keep it clean and dry. To keep it clean, dab some rubbing alcohol on a sterile cotton ball and apply to the area periodically to help prevent infection until the cord stump dries up and falls off, usually in ten days to three weeks. Hold off on submerging the navel area during bathing until this occurs. The withering cord stump will change color, from yellow to brown or black. This is normal, so don't worry.

Keep your daughter's diaper off the stump to avoid chafing. Most newborn disposable diapers now have an area cut out in the umbilical cord area to keep the diaper from rubbing against the cord. But if you do not have this kind of diaper, simply fold the diaper you have—whether disposable or cloth—below the navel

WHEN TO CALL THE DOCTOR

You should consult your daughter's doctor if the navel area becomes reddened, is oozing puss, or if a foul odor or discharge develops.

area. If the baby's diaper or clothing should stick to the stump, do not pull it off. First wet the area with warm water to loosen the grip. Then gently lift the material away from the area.

DIAPERING 101

If you've never diapered a baby before, the task can be intimidating. Don't worry. This is one skill that you get to practice over and over again, making you a pro in a very short time. The people who count this kind of thing say you're likely to change your daughter's diaper three thousand times! So don't be afraid; jump right in.

Think safety first. Always have everything you need at hand *before* you begin diapering. You cannot leave your daughter alone on a changing table for even a second while you turn away to reach for a new diaper. Have at hand warm water and sterile cotton or a clean face cloth, diaper ointment, and a clean diaper. Also, make sure your daughter is on a secure surface and keep one hand on her at all times. (Even newborns move in unpredictable ways.)

To begin diapering, lay your daughter on her back. If you are right-handed, her feet should be to your right side, her head to your left. If you are left-handed, place her feet to your left and her head to your right. This puts your dominant hand near the diaper area and free to do all the work. Unfasten the soiled diaper. Then, holding both of her ankles securely in one hand (the nondominant hand, which is closest to her head), lift your daughter's legs and bottom up off the surface. With your other hand remove the soiled diaper and wash her bottom.

You'll be surprised to see that your newborn's bowel movements (BMs) do not look like yours. Watery, greenish, or yellow-colored BMs are perfectly normal in infants for about the first three months. You might see small, hard "rabbit pellets" if your daughter is constipated. If she has diarrhea, it may look like water. Black, tarlike BMs are not healthy and should be reported to her doctor.

If the diaper is heavily soiled, you can wipe her bottom with the clean part of the diaper front to remove some excess. Then wash the bottom and genital area with a sterile cotton ball or washcloth dipped in warm water. Commercial baby wipes are too harsh for a newborn's skin, so stick with water for the first month or two.

At first, your newborn will require very frequent changes. After a few weeks, she will require fewer changes. That's when you can get better organized into a routine. Some babies move their bowels as they are eating; others will wait a while afterwards. Still others will be soiled before they even begin a feeding. Once you know when your daughter is likely to have a BM, you'll know when to be prepared with clean diapers.

Cloth Diapers: If you choose to use cloth diapers rather than disposables, and do not use a diaper cleaning service, you must be very careful to clean them thoroughly. When you remove a soiled diaper from your daughter, empty any bowel movement into the toilet immediately. Then put the diapers into a diaper pail that's partially filled with water. Wash the diapers in a separate wash load with a mild soap or detergent.

Diaper Rash: Babies wear diapers all day long, and even the most conscientious parent will eventually face diaper rash. The problem can be prevented somewhat by following these guidelines:

☐ Change diapers often. Be especially quick to remove a diaper soiled by a bowel movement.

DIAPERING TIPS

If you're using cloth diapers these quick tips can make the job easier:

• Keep the diapers unstained by adding one-half cup of Borax per gallon of water to the diaper pail.

• When washing diapers, don't use too much soap or detergent; too much is hard to rinse out thoroughly and the leftover can irritate a baby's bottom.

• Do not use fabric softener because this reduces the diaper's absorbency.

• Store the diaper pins by sticking them in a bar of soap. You'll always know where they are and the soap helps the pin slide more easily into the diaper.

□ Wrap diapers loosely. The new form-fitting disposables let very little air on your daughter's bottom, so try not to put them on too tightly.

□ Ease up on vigorous cleanings. Your daughter's bottom is delicate. Too much rubbing and/or harsh soap can be very irritating.

□ Change diapering products. If your daughter's rash keeps coming back, try different diapers, soaps, ointments, powders, etc. She may be allergic to one of these products.

Even with the best preventative tactics, it's likely your daughter will have diaper rash occasionally. When this happens, here are some ways to ease the pain:

□ Air out your baby's bottom. If at all possible, let your daughter be totally free of a diaper and any ointment for a few hours each day. If that's not possible, cut away the elasticized leg opening of the disposable diapers to allow air to circulate. Air is a great healer.

□ Soak her in a tub of barely warm water. Do not use soap! This adds to the irritation.

□ Apply diaper ointment liberally. This will help keep urine off the sore bottom.

□ Do not use baby wipes to clean after each bowel movement. These can be very irritating to the sensitive skin.

Most rashes will go away in a few days. If your daughter's rash will not heal or is causing fever or loss of appetite, call her doctor. Sometimes severe rashes require antibiotics and mediated ointments.

Diapering Baby Girls: Little girls have special diapering needs. Here are a few tips for girls only:

☐ To avoid vaginal infections, always wipe your daughter's bottom from the front to the back. This will keep the bowel movement from entering the vagina, which can cause an infection.

☐ Don't use talc with baby girls. It is associated with cervical cancer in later life. Cornstarch-based powders are a better choice.

☐ If using cloth diapers, fold the cloth to give extra padding in the back where the urine is likely to travel to.

BATHTIME!

Although careful cleaning of your daughter's diaper area is very important, she doesn't need a full body bath very often. In fact, most pediatricians agree that your newborn should only have sponge baths during her first week or two, until the stump of her umbilical cord falls off and the navel heals over. Then, a bath two or three times a week in the first year is sufficient. More bathing may dry out her delicate skin.

When you do give your daughter a sponge bath, get yourself

prepared before you bring her to the water. Gather together a basin of warm water, a clean washcloth, mild baby soap, and one or two towels or blanket in the room where you want to bathe her. To test the water temperature, stick your elbow in it; it should feel warm, not hot or cold.

Pick a warm room and any surface that's flat and comfortable for you both, such as a changing table, floor, or counter next to the sink. If the surface is hard, lay down a towel or blanket. If she is not on the floor, use a safety strap or keep one hand on her at all times to make sure she doesn't fall.

Undress the baby and wrap her in a towel, exposing only the part of her body you are washing at the moment. First, wash her face with a dampened washcloth without soap. Then wet the cloth again and wash the rest of her body. Pay special attention to creases under her arms, behind the ears, around the neck, and the genital area. Once you have washed those areas, make sure they are dry.

Into the tub: Once the umbilical cord stump has fallen off and the navel has healed, you can try placing your daughter directly in the water. Her first baths should be gentle and brief. If she seems miserable, go back to sponge baths for a week or two, then try the bath again.

Many parents like bathing their newborn in a special baby tub, the sink, or a plastic tub lined with a clean towel. Whatever type you use, fill the basin (before you place her inside) with two inches of warm water, testing it with your elbow. If you're filling the basin from the tap, turn the cold water on first and off last to avoid scalding the baby or yourself. Make sure your hot-water heater is set no higher than 120° F.

Have your supplies on hand and the room warm before bringing in your daughter. You will need a clean washcloth, mild baby soap, and one or two towels, plus a cup for rinsing with clean water. If your daughter has hair, you may want to have baby shampoo, too.

Once you've undressed your daughter, place her in the water right away so she doesn't get chilled. Use one of your hands to support her head and the other to guide her body in, feet first. Talk gently to her and slowly lower the rest of her body until she's in the tub. Most of her body and face should be well above the water level for safety, so you'll need to pour warm water over her body frequently to keep her warm.

Use a soft cloth to wash her face and hair, shampooing once or twice a week. Massage her scalp gently, including the area over her fontanels (soft spots). Don't worry. You won't hurt her by doing this. When you rinse the soap or shampoo from her head, cup your hand across her forehead so the suds run toward the sides, not into her eyes. If you get soap in her eyes, take the wet washcloth and wipe her eyes with lots of lukewarm water until the suds are gone. She will then open her eyes again. When your daughter comes out of the bath, wrap her in a towel, making sure her head is covered. Baby towels with hoods are very handy for this move.

The most important rule of baby bathing is this: If you have forgotten something or need to answer the phone or door during the bath, take the baby with you. *Never leave a baby alone in a bath*.

After a while, you and your daughter may find that bathtime is the best time of day. It's a chance for both of you to enjoy the soothing effects of water and to give each other your undivided attention.

Medical Care

Baby girls are precious and soft, but your daughter is far sturdier than she first appears. Still, she does need you to look after her health and give her continued medical care and checkups.

ROUTINE AT-HOME HEALTH CARE

Keeping your newborn healthy is a top priority in the first few months. The best way to do that is to limit your daughter's exposure to illness. The immune system of newborns is less mature and developed than that of older children and adults. Because of this immature immune system, it's a good idea to limit your daughter's exposure to lots of visitors in the first weeks.

SUNBURN ALERT

During the first six months, an infant is extremely sensitive to sun and sunburn, so keep your daughter out of direct and reflected sunlight (such as off concrete, water, or sand), especially during the peak sunlight hours of 10 A.M. to 4 P.M. Dress her in lightweight, light-colored clothing with a bonnet or hat to shade her face. If she's lying or sitting in one place, make sure it is in the shade and adjust her position as the sun moves. If you must take her into sunlight, definitely use sunblock to protect her skin.

Ask your daughter's doctor when it is appropriate to take the baby into crowds, such as the mall. Stuffy stores and crowded spaces are breeding places for germs, so it's usually best to stay far away for the first few weeks. Also, if friends or relatives have a cold or infection, ask them to delay visiting until they are better. If you, your partner, or a sibling becomes ill, of course it is harder (or impossible) to keep the baby from being exposed. But, if possible, limit the sick person's contact with your daughter so this person doesn't cough in her face or kiss the baby until they've recovered. Everyone in the household should practice good hygiene by washing their hands thoroughly before touching the baby.

ROUTINE MEDICAL CHECKUPS

Keeping your baby girl healthy is very important in these first three months. To do this, you'll need to give her ongoing professional medical care, so make sure you keep those doctor appointments for her checkups.

Stephen Muething, M.D., associate director of clinical services for the division of General Pediatrics at Cincinnati Children's Hospital Medical Center, says that babies generally receive routine medical checkups twice in their first three months: often at one week and then again at two months. To get the most out of these visits, Dr. Muething recommends that you prepare in advance. "I'm a big believer in the assertive parent," he says. "Write down your questions and concerns. You're probably going to be feeling tired. The baby may start crying during the exam. The doctor may be rushed, and with all that's going on, it's hard to remember what information you want to take home with you. Don't just go with the doctor's agenda during the visit and remain passive. Families who get more bang for their buck go in saying, 'This is what we need to know during this visit: We have these three questions and we need to talk to you about this.' "

One-week exam: When you take your daughter for her first medical checkup, consider it a good opportunity to learn more about your child's health and to begin to get to know her doctor.

Either before or during this visit, you'll be asked a long list of questions that will help the doctor better care for your newborn.

The first group of questions will pertain to prenatal history. The doctor may ask questions such as: What was the pregnancy like? Did you have any health problems? Did you get regular prenatal care? Did you take any prescription medications or over-the-counter drugs? Did you drink alcoholic beverages (including beer or wine) and if so, how much? Did you smoke during pregnancy? Did you use any drugs like marijuana or cocaine? (Don't feel insulted by any of these questions. You should doubt the competency of a doctor who *doesn't* ask them.)

You will then be asked about the birth experience. The doctor may ask: Was the baby full-term or premature? If premature, how many weeks early was she born? How much did she weigh? Were there any signs of fetal distress during birth? How was she delivered (vaginally, by cesarean, with forceps, or a vacuum extractor)? How long did labor and delivery take? At birth, did the baby need any help breathing? Did she need to spend any time in a special care unit or the neonatal intensive care unit (NICU)? Did she need treatment for jaundice? How long did she stay in the hospital? Did the doctor who examined her in the hospital tell you of any problems? (If you did not give birth to your daughter—if she is adopted or you are providing foster care—the doctor will ask you for any information you have about her birth and prenatal history, and about the biological family's medical history.)

The doctor may also want to know about the baby's life at home. He may ask: How is the baby doing with the main newborn activities—eating, sleeping, pooping, and peeing? When does she sleep and for how long? Where does she sleep? Do you always put her to sleep on her back, the safest position to prevent SIDS? How many wet diapers does she have each day? How often does she have bowel movements? How is the rest of the family doing? Do you feel comfortable taking care of the baby? Are you and your partner having any conflicts over her care? Are you getting any sleep? How is your mood (happy, elated, stressed, depressed, etc.)? Do you get support from family, friends, or hired care-givers? And so on.

With this information in mind, the doctor will turn his attention to your daughter and give her a complete going over. He will double-check to make sure that nothing unusual was missed in the hospital such as a cleft lip, ear abnormalities, or heart murmur. He will also take a bit of blood to see if the baby has jaundice. (Jaundice gives the skin a yellowish color; it is caused by excess bilirubin, a by-product of old red blood cells.)

The doctor will then begin the physical exam. He or the nurse will weigh your daughter and measure her length and head circumference. He may also take her vital signs (heart rate, breathing rate, and temperature) and record them on her medical chart. Then the doctor will give your daughter a thorough physical.

☐ He listens to the baby's heart and lungs with a stethoscope.

☐ He examines her abdomen, checking to see that the umbilical cord is not getting infected and that the naval (belly button) is healing well. A few days after the cord has fallen off, normal skin should have grown over the navel. If not, the doctor may swab on some silver nitrate to help it heal. He feels your daughter's abdomen to be sure that it is soft, not tender, and has no unexpected masses. While feeling her belly, he checks that her liver, kidneys, and spleen are not enlarged.

☐ He makes sure her hip joints are developing properly. He looks to see that the skin creases on both thighs are the same. Then he pushes the baby's hips down into the table and rotates them, moving the knees outward and down toward the table. If he feels the joints slip, she may have a condition called developmental dysplasia of the hip.

☐ He checks your daughter's femoral pulses (the pulses between the thigh and the abdomen) to make sure there is good blood flow from the heart to the lower half of the body.

☐ He examines her legs, feet, and overall skin color and condition.

☐ He examines the genitals. He checks to see that the labia (the folds of skin surrounding the opening of the vagina) are normal. He will also reassure you that if you see a mucosy vaginal discharge and sometimes a small amount of bleeding from the vagina that it is nothing to worry about. This discharge that may last for a week or so is due to the effects of hormones transferred from the mother before birth.

☐ He examines the head, noting the shape and feel of the fontanels, the "soft spots" where the bony plates of the skull have not yet joined.

☐ He checks her suck and gag reflexes. (Your daughter should suck when something is placed in the front of her mouth and gag when something is placed toward the back of her throat.)

☐ He examines her eyes to see if they are aligned, checks the position of the ears, and looks inside at the eardrums.

At this first visit, the doctor will also focus on your daughter's feeding. He may ask questions such as: How often does she eat? How long does she nurse at the breast, or how much formula does she take? Have you had any nursing problems? Does she seem satisfied after eating? The doctor will also want to make sure that you're comfortable with your chosen method of feeding, be it breast or bottle.

Two-month visit: In addition to a thorough physical, the doctor may also check your daughter's reflexes at the two-month visit. Some that may be examined include:

☐ **The startle (or Moro) reflex.** A loud or sudden noise should make your daughter stretch her arms and legs out, then draw her arms back into her chest.

□ **The step and place reflex.** If held as if she's "standing" on a flat surface, your daughter will lift her legs as if taking steps. If held so the tops of her feet are dragging against a surface (such as the underside of a table), she'll lift her legs as if to step up onto the surface.

□ **The Babinski reflex.** If the sole of the foot is stroked from heel to toe, your daughter stretches her toes up and fans them out (the opposite of what older children and adults do, which is to curl their toes down).

The doctor also checks how your daughter is developing. He does this by asking you questions, watching the baby, and interacting with her. He may check her development while doing the physical exam, or he may do a developmental exam separately. He is checking things such as:

□ Does she watch people's faces? Can she make eye contact?

□ Does she move both arms and both legs equally?

□ Does she make any sounds besides crying?

□ Does she follow an object with her eyes as it moves from the side of her visual field to the midpoint?

□ If she is placed on her stomach can she raise her head? If so, how far?

Again, at the two-month-checkup, be sure to come prepared to ask questions and tell the doctor about your concerns. Most doctor visits last less than 12 minutes, so being organized can help you get the most out of that time.

PHONE CALLS TO THE DOCTOR

Many doctors have phone hours when you can call with routine questions. In some practices, a nurse or nurse practitioner may handle most of these calls unless you specifically want or need to talk to the doctor. Don't hesitate to call with your concerns, no matter how small they may seem. Of course, if you suspect your daughter is ill and may need prompt attention, don't wait for phone hours—call your doctor immediately.

Calls for Emergencies: If your daughter has any of the following conditions, call 911 or your doctor immediately, or go to the emergency room:

- ☐ trouble breathing
- ☐ head injury with loss of consciousness, vomiting, or blue or pale skin color
- ☐ bleeding that won't stop
- ☐ poisoning
- ☐ seizures
- ☐ sudden loss of energy or ability to move
- ☐ high fever

☐ bloody urine

☐ bloody diarrhea

☐ any fever or abnormal behavior in a child under three months

---

COMMON INFANT HEALTH CONCERNS

In the first three months of life, your infant daughter will give you plenty to wonder and worry about. The health concerns that many parents fret over include jaundice, hemangiomas, colic, and SIDS. Here are the facts:

Jaundice: Jaundice, which causes yellowing of the skin and whites of the eyes, is quite common in newborns. It is caused by a buildup of bilirubin in the blood, a substance produced by the normal breakdown of red blood cells. Usually bilirubin passes through the

---

FEVER CONCERN

"Doctors are more concerned about fever in the first two months than they will be for the rest of the child's life. Most doctors say that if your daughter has a fever of 100.5° F or above, call. Even if you're an experienced parent, even if you think the baby looks okay—call."
—Dr. Stephen Muething

liver and is excreted as bile through the intestines. But sometimes it builds up faster than a newborn can pass from her body.

If bilirubin levels begin to climb too high after birth, and if the baby is born in a hospital, treatment with phototherapy begins right away before dangerous levels are reached. The baby is placed unclothed under blue or broad-spectrum white light until bilirubin levels fall. The light alters the bilirubin so that it is more rapidly excreted by the liver. If your daughter is already home when it emerges, she may be treated with a portable light unit or she may need to return to the hospital.

Hemangiomas: Hemangiomas are large, noncancerous, blood-filled, usually red birthmarks that affect about 10 percent of all infants by age one and are more common in infant girls. They are especially common in low birth weight, premature infants.

Hemangiomas are caused by an abnormality in the blood vessels and occur most frequently on the face and neck. They usually do

IMMUNIZATION SCHEDULE

At your daughter's routine medical checkups, she will receive a series of immunization shots from birth through eighteen months. Be sure to follow your doctor's instructions on when to bring your daughter in for her immunizations and check out the current recommended immunization schedule on the website of the American Academy of Pediatrics at www.aap.org or the Centers For Disease Control at www.cdc.gov/nip/acip.

not pose a major threat to the child's health, but because the birth-marks are prominent and may be unsightly, you may find them very upsetting. Only a small portion of hemangiomas require treatment, and most will resolve themselves before your daughter reaches school age.

Colic: Some babies cry much more than others. There is no calming them, no rocking them to sleep, no relief for the parents. If your daughter is a crier, check with your doctor. She may have colic.

Colic is the extreme end of normal crying behavior in a baby between three weeks and three months of age. In a baby with colic, the crying lasts longer (more than three hours a day), occurs more often (more than three days a week), and is more intense than expected for the baby's age.

As I quickly learned with my colicky middle baby, it is very difficult to console a baby once an episode of colic has started. The baby may seem to be in pain, flailing and screaming, with tense legs drawn up to her belly. But the crying is not due to hunger, a wet diaper, or other visible causes, and the child cannot be calmed down.

Why do these babies cry so much? Your parents and grandparents may tell you that colic is caused by gastrointestinal problems such as stomach pain due to gas in the intestine and digestive problems such as milk allergies. But modern medicine now says it is not a disease. Today, evidence suggests that colic is due to the baby's temperament and an inability to regulate crying. A baby's temperament may make her extremely sensitive to the environment, and she reacts to the environment or changes to the environment by crying. The baby's nervous system is immature, which results in her being unable to calm down once the crying starts.

Although the parents of every crying baby suspect colic, only approximately 10 to 30 percent of babies actually cry long and often enough to wear the medical term. It is equally common among male and female babies, and in those who are breast-fed and bottle-fed.

Fortunately, babies with colic grow and develop normally. They are just as likely as other children to be healthy and happy. (It's my own sanity I came to worry about!) In most cases, colic goes away on its own in about three months.

Dealing with colic. If your daughter's doctor has confirmed that she is perfectly healthy and has no physical reason for her frequent crying, the best you can do is to use a trial-and-error method to find ways to calm the screams.

When she is fed, rested, and diapered, you can try any of the calming strategies mapped out earlier in this chapter. In addition, you might find, as I did, that there is peace in constant motion: walk or rock her; put her in the swing or infant seat; sing songs and dance around the room; place her across your lap on her belly and rub her back while you sway your legs; put her in the car or stroller and take her for a ride—anything is worth a try.

Often, despite your best efforts, your colicky baby will continue to cry. When that happens, it's *sooooo* frustrating—enough to make you wonder why you ever thought it would be a good idea to have this baby in the first place. That's when it's time to step back and try to salvage your sanity. Here are a few strategies that worked for me:

Don't blame yourself. There are far too many factors involved to take sole responsibility for colic. Neither you nor your spouse should let these periods of crying convince you that you are inadequate parents. While your infant is wailing, remind yourself over and over again that this is not your fault. You have done nothing to cause the crying. You are a good parent.

Expect the crying. If your daughter has colic, one thing you can count on is that she won't skip an evening of screaming. Don't plan to have dinner, or visitors, or quiet conversations during her usual crying time. Plan to spend the colic period practicing soothing tactics.

Take a break. You can't stand on your eyelashes to calm your child for three hours on end without becoming overwhelmed with anger. You will need time away. Encourage your spouse to share the responsibility by taking turns using soothing tactics, and arrange for a sitter on a regular basis so you can both get some much-needed time away from your daughter. As odd as it sounds, the growth of a positive relationship with a colicky baby may depend on how often you can get away from her to calm down by taking a walk, visiting a friend, or sitting in a bath.

Don't forget that colic is temporary. Like pregnancy, colic, too, is a stage of growth and development that will end. Typically the crying periods peak at six weeks of age and then taper off by three months. Eventually, all children grow out of colic.

Remember that crying will not hurt your daughter. This is perhaps the hardest lesson of all to learn because it is so difficult for parents to let their babies cry, even when it is apparent that nothing is going to stop it.

SUDDEN INFANT DEATH SYNDROME (SIDS)

For all parents, SIDS is an unspeakable fear because it is the leading cause of death in the postneonatal period (one month to one year). SIDS is a mysterious syndrome in which seemingly healthy babies go to sleep and are found dead—for no apparent reason.

By definition, SIDS is the sudden death of an infant under one year that is unexplained even after a thorough investigation. The American Academy of Pediatrics says that the occurrence of SIDS is rare during the first month of life, increases to a peak between two and four months and then declines.

The good news is that SIDS is relatively rare, striking fewer than three thousand babies a year, and getting rarer. Rates have declined by 50 percent since 1992 when the American Academy of Pediatrics began to recommend that healthy babies be put to sleep on their backs.

Why should sleeping position make such a difference? Some speculate that when babies sleep on their stomachs the air they exhale may get trapped in folds of bedding. The babies then may rebreathe this air, which is low in oxygen and high in carbon dioxide. Rising levels of carbon dioxide should wake a baby, who might cry, cough or move his or her head enough to get more fresh air. But some babies fail to wake, perhaps because their brain function is immature or abnormal.

If this theory is correct, it may describe just one of several causes of the mysterious deaths. Researchers have identified other factors, besides stomach sleeping, that seem to increase the risk of SIDS. These include: sleeping on a soft surface; overheating; a mother's smoking during pregnancy; exposure to smoke after birth; late or no prenatal care; premature birth or low birth weight; or being male.

Based on these findings, the American Academy of Pediatrics and other authorities suggest some ways likely to reduce the risk of SIDS:

☐ Healthy newborns, including most premature newborns, should be put to sleep on their backs.

☐ Make sure that all caregivers understand that your daughter must sleep on her back. Stomach sleeping used to be standard in the United States, and many grandparents and babysitters still tuck babies in on their stomachs.

☐ When babies are awake, they should spend time on their stomachs so they can work on controlling their heads, pushing themselves up, and other feats of infant strength and coordination. This waking "tummy time" also may help prevent flat spots from developing on the back of a baby's head. (Another way to prevent flattening is to make sure an infant's head is in different positions when she lies in the crib. If your daughter usually turns her head to the right to see the doorway or a mobile, change her orientation so she has to look left to see it. Or move the mobile. In any case, these flat spots are temporary and do no damage.)

☐ If your daughter can roll from her back to her stomach, but can't roll back, you should roll her back. Once she can roll from her stomach to her back, you can let her sleep in whatever position she assumes after you put her down on her back.

☐ The recommendation that babies sleep on their backs may not apply to some children with certain medical conditions. Your health-care provider can advise you on which position is best for your daughter.

Physical Growth

Your daughter is growing by leaps and bounds every day. She is gaining weight and growing in length at amazing speed. If she is feeding regularly without excessive vomiting or fussiness, she will grow as expected and right on track according to standard growth charts.

GROWTH CHART

In Appendix A you'll find out how to access the growth charts your daughter's doctor uses to keep track of her weight and length. You can plot your big girl's growth on these charts. Just keep in mind that they are general averages and your daughter is unique. Always talk to your doctor about any growth concerns you have and use the charts only as a guide to compare your daughter with typical growth patterns.

Your Girl's Developing Senses

The parts of the brain that process information from the sense of touch are more developed at birth than those involved in vision or hearing. So it's touch that first gives your daughter a way to judge and react to her surroundings. Touch also gives her an emotional sense of security, and in this way becomes a most important component in the bonding process.

Although touching your daughter is unavoidable in day-to-day care, that's not the only kind of touch she needs. Take time to stroke your daughter's skin while bathing and diapering. Learn more about the art of baby massage as a way of improving your connection with her. And keep in mind that each baby is unique in the way she processes stimulation. Some will immediately cuddle and coo and obviously enjoy being handled and stroked; others will stiffen and arch their backs and show other signs of being a noncuddler. Experimentation and practice will help you find when and how you can touch your daughter in ways that will make you both feel comfortable and attached.

Emotional Development

Your baby girl's physical health is certainly a top priority, but don't overlook the importance of nurturing her emotional health as well. To do this for your newborn, give her lots of love. Giving our children love enables them to value and love themselves. It teaches them how to love and relate to other people. And it allows them to become emotionally stable people. This strong emotional development begins at birth and continues throughout childhood through the process of bonding and attachment.

BONDING WITH YOUR BABY GIRL

Child psychologists tell us that it is very important to bond with our babies so they can develop strong emotional attachments to us and become secure and confident adults. I'm sure this is absolutely true, but I've always found the word *bonding* to be a bit misleading. It gives the impression of an epoxy glue–type union that, in a moment's time, adheres two together forever. Child psychologists tell us that's not really what bonding is all about. Human bonding is a gradual process that begins before a child's birth and continues throughout childhood.

Some believe that there is a "critical" bonding period immediately after birth. This notion leaves many new parents feeling guilty and depressed when in the moments after childbirth they feel little more than exhaustion and a vague sense of fondness toward the newly arrived child. Quite commonly, truthful women admit, "I thought it would be love at first sight, but when I first looked at my daughter, 'love' was hardly my reaction." This idea of instant bonding is also quite upsetting to adoptive parents who are not available to the child immediately after birth. It's equally distressing to parents who are separated from their babies because either the baby or the mother needs prompt medical care.

Fortunately for those parents who worry they've missed their chance to form a lasting attachment to their child, bonding does not happen in an instantaneous and magical moment. It happens each day in the routine interactions between a parent and a child—

not in the perfunctory acts of feeding and changing diapers, but in the smiles, coos, and moments of eye contact that occur during these activities. It happens as parents learn about and respond to their baby's patterns, temperament, likes and dislikes, and unique daily rhythms. And it happens as babies become aware of their parents' smell, sound, and touch.

Bonding doesn't occur instantly, but it is very important that the process does occur. A secure parent/child relationship forms the basis for all later emotional attachments and it lays the groundwork that will enable your daughter to seek and achieve loving and secure relationships in adult life. Emotional attachment also contributes to her overall mental and physical growth. Studies repeatedly find that babies who are deprived of the opportunity for emotional attachment are at risk for suffering the failure to thrive syndrome. This is a collection of symptoms that occur for no apparent physical reason. They include loss of weight, failure to grow, and a disruption in physical and mental development. When later cared for by emotionally involved and loving caretakers who give the babies an opportunity to form a loving relationship, these infants resume normal mental and physical development.

Like any love relationship, bonding develops in gradual stages and improves and deepens with time and attention. To nurture that bonding process with your infant try these three simple ideas suggested in the book *Ages and Stages*, which I wrote with Dr. Charles E. Schaefer:

☐ Consistently and immediately respond to your daughter's cries of distress.

☐ Give plenty of physical contact. Babies feel safer, sleep better, gain more weight, and are more interested in being with people when they are often cuddled, held, and stroked. The importance of loving touch cannot be overemphasized.

☐ Play with your daughter. Even in the first few months of life, infants enjoy games like peek-a-boo and songs. This creates a pleasure bond that encourages affection and attachment.

DADDY'S LITTLE GIRL

If the new dad in your house is keeping his distance from his newborn daughter, he's probably feeling an uncertainty that strikes many dads. He's looking at this precious child and thinking: *I have no idea how to relate to this tiny female.* Some dads will easily throw their infant sons up into the air, but will balk at the thought of even holding a little girl. They see her as too fragile, somehow "foreign," and so keep their distance. Even though this fear of infant females affects many men, Daddy's little girl needs the male in her

IT'S ALL IN THE BRAIN

The cerebral cortex contains neurons that influence intelligence, memory, and interprets sensory input. This region is thicker in females on the left side of the brain, making females more left-brain dominant. The left side of the brain is associated with verbal skills such as speaking, reading, and writing. These are skills that females usually excel in throughout life.

life to hold her and love her; she needs to feel his admiration for her abilities and know he is interested in her. These feelings help her make a secure attachment that will last a lifetime.

Alice Sterling Honig, Ph.D., professor emerita of child and family studies in the College of Human Services and Health Professions at Syracuse University and a Fellow of the American Psychological Association and the Society for Research in Child Development, has studied parent/child bonding. She's noticed that it's sometimes more difficult for new dads to bond with their daughters than with their sons. "I used to present a film to my students," Honig remembers, "that showed a big, truck-driver father being taught by a very efficient nurse in the hospital how to bathe his infant daughter. The nurse was giving him good directions on bathing techniques, but the fearful look on his face and the tension in his muscles made it obvious that she was not giving all the information he needed. Dads need to know that baby girls are sturdy (in fact, physically, they are often sturdier than boys). Dads need to be assured that little girls won't break with careful handling, and they need lots of positive encouragement when they do make the effort to get close to and provide for their daughters."

So dads, don't hold back. Take your baby girl in your arms, stroke her cheek with your finger, and talk to her. Strike up a conversation, sing her song, tell her about your workday. You'll find she's a wonderful listener who will hang on every word you say. She will gaze into your eyes with unconditional devotion. This is just too precious an experience for you to miss and it offers the added bonus of helping your little girl grow secure and confident.

Cognitive Development

There is no telling how far your little girl will go in this world of equal opportunity. To give her every advantage, be sure to stimulate her intellectual growth. Did you know that your daughter's brain grows and develops faster during this first year than at any other time in her life? Don't miss this opportunity to encourage cognitive development. But no need to rush out and buy expensive or high-tech toys at this early stage. Talking and singing to your daughter and playing games with her fingers and toes are fun and effective ways to boost brain power.

GAMES BABY GIRLS LOVE

Your newborn looks like she's ready for action as her arms and legs move, kick, and punch the air. But these motions are simply reflexes that she cannot consciously start or stop. Fine motor skills that will allow your daughter to grab hold of her toys to explore and play will develop in an orderly progression but at an uneven pace filled with rapid spurts and harmless delays. You can help you daughter develop the fine motor skills so important to her growth and development through infant games and play.

The hands of a newborn are closed most of the time. Like the rest of her body, she has little control over them. But in a wonderful innate reflex, if you touch her palm, she will unconsciously open her hand and clutch your finger. This reflex disappears within two to three months. During this time your daughter will also grasp at any object placed in her hand, but without any awareness that she is doing so. Then, the fist will relax and she will drop the object, still unaware of what she has done. But it's all part of her developing abilities. By two weeks, she may begin flailing at objects that interest her (although she can't yet grasp them without your help). That's a good time to play with your daughter by showing her a brightly colored toy with strong, contrasting colors. Hold it just out of reach and watch her focus on it and then begin to wave her arms and move her legs in excitement. Bring the object down to her hand and let her grab on. If you give her a baby rattle, for example, she will clutch and shake it with vigor (although not with intentional will) and then suddenly drop it as her hand opens.

By eight weeks, although she still has not developed a deliberate grasp, your daughter will begin to discover and play with her hands. Using the sense of touch alone, she will explore her fingers and bring them to her mouth for further investigation. The mouth has many nerve endings, making it an ideal tool for learning.

At three months, she will add the sense of sight to her daily "play" and stare at her fingers in absolute awe. With fascination, she will watch them move and wiggle for long stretches of time. At this age, her own hands may be her favorite toy.

When hand-eye coordination begins to develop between two and four months, your daughter will discover the joy of focusing on an object and reaching out to intentionally grab it. Once in hand, it will immediately go to her mouth for further exploration.

Your newborn's escalating alertness allows more time for active play as the weeks go on. Try a few different things to see what she enjoys and responds to. Show her rattles and demonstrate how they can make noise. Play with textured objects such as stuffed an-

MOM AND DAD PLAY STYLES

Right from infancy, moms and dads have different play styles. As researchers observed parents playing with their infants, they found that moms often contain the babies' movements by holding their legs or hips, and calmed them with a soft voice, slow speech, and repeated rhythmic phrases. Fathers, on the other hand, often poke their babies, pedal their legs, make loud, abrupt noises, and stimulate their babies to higher pitches of excitement.

imals, guiding her hands to touch them. Gently tickle and kiss her tummy and feet. Hold a rattle or small toy in front of her and allow her to track it with her eyes.

By three months, your daughter will be ready for some traditional baby games. This is when games that repeat a sequence of rhyming words are especially fun. In a singsongy voice, try "Pat-a-Cake," "Row Row Row Your Boat," and "Ring Around the Rosey."

It's important to respect your daughter's feelings about playtime. When she is hungry, tired, or uncomfortable, meet those needs first before attempting to play. And pace your games according to her reactions. Keep going only as long as she remains interested and stop when she seems to have had enough.

EARLY LANGUAGE DEVELOPMENT

They say that females love to talk. That may be a stereotype, but getting your newborn to "talk" to you as often as possible will indeed help to give her the gift of gab. Although your little girl may have no idea what you're saying, take time to talk with her every day. Ask questions. Pause for answer time. Loosen up. Laugh. Joke. Enjoy. Don't make the mistake of shying away from baby talk. It's a wonderful way to entertain, educate, and love your daughter. And you'll probably never find such an eager listener ever again!

STAGES OF INFANT LANGUAGE DEVELOPMENT

As in most other areas of development, babies learn language at different rates and in different ways. Some coo pleasantly; others grunt and squeak. Some babble incessantly; others listen intently. But along the way, you'll find these general signs of language growth:

Newborns listen to your voice. Vocalize by crying. Enjoy listening to music and your singing.

One- to three-month-olds coo pleasantly. Make mostly vowel sounds. Will initiate communication, repeat sounds, and respond when given the opportunity.

Here are a few simple guidelines to encourage early language development:

☐ **Try to eliminate background noise like the TV or radio.** It's difficult for an infant to concentrate on your voice when there are other sounds to listen to.

☐ **Use a higher than usual pitch in a singsong manner.** Studies show that high-pitched sounds attract an infant's attention and melodic intonation keeps that attention longer than normal adult conversational tone.

☐ **Speak slowly, and use simple words and short sentences.** In casual conversation, many adults tend to slur words and run one sentence into the next. Speaking clearly and simply will help your daughter become accustomed to the sounds of specific words and basic sentence structures.

☐ **Engage your daughter's interest in conversation** by keeping your face about twelve inches from her, using an animated style, and changing your facial expressions.

☐ **When you talk to your daughter, pause occasionally as if waiting for a response.** Ask questions and allow a few moments of silence to pass before continuing the conversation. These "conversations" teach lessons about tone, pacing, and taking turns when talking to someone else. As early as one month of age, you may be surprised to hear a cooing response.

Social Development

Your daughter may not be ready yet for playdates, but she is still a very social being. You can help her get to know her family and her world by providing her with early opportunities for separation experiences and social stimulation.

STEPS TOWARD SEPARATION

Your daughter may begin to show just how much she loves you—and only you—as early as three months of age. As your daughter learns to distinguish herself from others, she may cry at the sight of unfamiliar faces, and she may reject people who look different than you—eyeglasses or a beard will send some babies into hysterics.

All mentally healthy children will go through a period of separation anxiety. But you can lessen the degree of upset by taking some preparatory steps while your daughter is still in infancy.

Once your daughter is one month old, create regular opportunities for separation. Call upon willing relatives, find a reliable sitter, or trade sitting time with another mother so you can leave your daughter at least once a week for one- to two-hour periods. This will establish a comfortable routine for your daughter and will also give you time to schedule weekly dates with your spouse, or do something else just for yourself. Starting this routine soon after birth has advantages because your daughter won't yet protest being left behind, and setting up regular separation time will help both you and her continue the schedule when she gets old enough to complain about your absence.

Separation "games" can help your daughter understand that when you leave, you also come back. When your daughter is old enough to notice when you enter and leave a room, leave the room for a brief period of time, but maintain voice contact. Then return directly to her with a playful tickle or cuddle. Over time, leave the room for increasingly longer periods to teach your daughter that just because you're out of sight, doesn't mean you've disappeared.

Peek-a-boo and hide-and-seek are also playful ways to teach the reassuring reality of object permanence.

If you find yourself feeling guilty or apprehensive at the thought of leaving your baby girl, you can ease your own separation anxiety by following these guidelines:

Find a capable sitter. Family members are the most desirable sitters, but sometimes they are not available on a regular basis and so you may need to find a competent, caring person you can count on. The more confidence you have in your sitter, the less worried you'll feel while you're gone.

Never sneak out. It's easier and faster to duck out the door when your daughter isn't looking, but it defeats the goal of easing separation anxiety. It's confusing and upsetting, even to an infant, to suddenly realize that you're not around and she has no idea where you are or if you'll be back. Let your daughter see you depart and later see you come back. It won't take long before she learns that leaving is not forever.

Stay calm. Emotions are contagious. Mothers who appear worried about separation pass this feeling on to their children. Don't prolong your goodbyes by rushing back for another kiss. Don't spend too much time sharing your forlorn expression and sorrowful tone of voice. Say goodbye cheerfully and then leave.

Although you can't eliminate the separation anxiety stage from your child's developmental calendar, early separation experiences can ease the upset of this trying time. They can also teach babies a valuable lesson: When Mom and Dad leave, babies can trust other adults until they return—and they always do return.

SOCIAL STIMULATION

Babies need to see, hear, and touch people to learn about their world and how they fit into it. So don't sequester your daughter in her quiet nursery; make her a part of your family right from the beginning. Bring her into the kitchen to watch you cook and prepare meals. Let her join you at dinner and listen to your social conversations. Let her partake in social gatherings, holiday parties, and outdoor excursions.

Your daughter's temperament will largely determine the degree of social stimulation she's ready for. Your daughter may love to be in the middle of things when she is awake—bring on the family and friends, and she's raring to go! Or you may notice that she

THE SQUEAKY WHEEL

Babies who make a lot of noise and complain when they're left alone, get the most social stimulation—they demand to be a part of the action at all times. On the other hand, quiet, "good" babies, who are content to lie in their cribs alone often miss out on necessary social stimulation. Of course, it's tempting to let silent babies lie, but your quiet daughter shouldn't miss out on social stimulation just because she's less demanding.

wants only small doses of excitement at certain times of the day. To find just the right degree of social stimulation that's best for your daughter, take your cues from her.

When she is ready for social interaction by three months of age, she will meet your gaze and smile, following you with her eyes as you come and go. She will reach toward you. She will become more alert when you speak to her. She'll also carefully watch and make noises in response to other things that interest her, such as toys, her own reflection in the mirror, or friendly visitors.

New babies can also let you know when they've had enough attention. Crying is the most obvious cue, but they also will sneeze, pass gas, or yawn when they need to shut down for a while. She may also turn her face away from you. These signs of irritability when you're trying to play and be social are not a rejection of you. They are your daughter's attempts to communicate the best she can.

Choosing Childcare

Once you hold your little girl in your arms and take in that sweet smell, you'll probably wish you never had to leave her side. But, returning to work shortly after the birth of the baby is a hard reality for many new moms. When that's the case, finding good childcare is a top priority. Finding just the right type of care can take much effort, but when you make arrangements that you trust, the peace of mind you get in return is well worth the time spent making the right choice.

Here are some guidelines to help you select the child-care arrangement that will be best for both you and your daughter.

CHOOSING A CAREGIVER

There are several types of child-care arrangements to choose from. These include in-home care, home-based care, and day-care centers. I have used all three at different times while raising my children and have found each has its good and bad points. So think about the pros and cons of every option before making your decision.

In-home Care: In-home care allows your daughter to stay in her own home with a sitter, which may be a family member, a nanny, or an au pair. This type of care gives you greater flexibility—you can accept overtime at work or attend late meetings and not worry about childcare arrangements. In-home care is also usually more personal and allows your daughter to stay at home without the jostling and inconvenience of being carried to and from another location in all sorts of weather. Another bonus is that your caregiver will likely take care of your child even when she is sick, which is usually out of the question at day-care facilities.

There is a downside to in-home care. It's usually the most expensive option (unless you've hired a family member). Also, if your caregiver becomes ill and cannot take care of your daughter, there's no backup. Finally, if you opt for a live-in nanny or au pair, you and your family may find that you lose some privacy at home.

Home-based Day-care: Home-based day-care provides care for a child in the caregiver's home, often with one adult supervising several children. The benefits include: small group size (usually), a more homelike setting, and flexibility of hours for the parents. Often it is less expensive than other options.

On the other hand, home-based day-care is not as strictly regulated as day-care centers are, and the laws on licensing differ from state to state. Also, many caregivers are not formally trained, although they often have young children of their own. And, if the caregiver is ill, parents are left without backup arrangements for their children.

Day-care Center: Day-care in a center, preschool, nursery school, or provided by your workplace, offers several advantages: It is more likely to be run in accordance with state regulations that set minimum standards for staff-child ratios, group size, staff training, and building safety. Additionally, day-care centers usually take children from six-week-old infants to school-age. Day-care providers usually have training in early childhood development, and a staff illness doesn't affect the reliable care of your daughter.

The disadvantages of day-care include: There are often waiting lists because of a limited number of licensed centers, they usually have a more structured environment for your child because of the focus on regulations, there is frequent turnover of staff, and you may encounter inflexible pick-up and drop-off times.

CHILDCARE CRITERIA CHECKLIST

While considering the types of childcare, remember there are different guidelines depending on the age of your daughter. For infant care, finding a completely trustworthy caretaker is critical because your daughter cannot tell you if she is being subjected to neglect or abusive behavior. If you're thinking about an out-of-home arrangement, visit the facility and look closely at these factors:

- ☐ Are all infants fed in the upright position as they should be?

- ☐ Are bottles propped up on pillows for feedings?

- ☐ Are all infants put to sleep lying on their backs?

- ☐ Are the caretakers engaged with the children—not sitting around just watching them (or the TV)?

- ☐ Are the children given lots of smiles and approval?

- ☐ Are infants separated from the older children (who might accidentally hurt them)?

- ☐ Is there an open-door policy on visits from parents?

- ☐ Are sick children mingled in with the rest?

If you've opted to hire an in-home caregiver such as a nanny, be thorough:

- ☐ Interview the applicants at least twice.

- ☐ Ask for several references and check them all.

- ☐ If the caregiver will be driving with your child, check her driving record.

- ☐ Outline all expected duties: hours, salary, paid vacation, and sick leave.

PLAN FOR EMERGENCIES

Be sure to give the caregiver all emergency contacts. Write down your work phone numbers, beeper numbers, cell phone numbers, and e-mail addresses. Make sure the caregiver knows what to do in an emergency and provide phone numbers of friends, relatives, and your daughter's physician.

Whether home-based or center-based, slowly ease your daughter into the new situation. Visit the center several times and leave her for short periods (if allowed) before leaving her for the entire day. Or, invite your new nanny or au pair over for lunch. Let her care for your daughter while you stay nearby to observe. Give your daughter the chance to get to know the nanny's voice and smell before you leave.

Leaving my babies behind in the care of another person was always very difficult. I'm not sure whether I suffered so because I worried about not being in control of my child's life, that something bad would happen while I was gone, or because I secretly feared that my baby would love the caregiver more than me. It was probably a combination of all three. But looking back, I realize that these caregivers were an essential link that helped me balance the responsibilities of my job and family. Happily, my children have grown up to be happy, stable people—no worse for their days in childcare.

Moving Through Girlhood

The first three months are quite an adventure for both you and your daughter. This is a time of getting to know each other, learning how to live peacefully together, and of course, for falling in love. You'll find the time passes very quickly, and before you know it, you'll be moving into the next stage of babyhood—the four- to seven-month period when your newborn turns into a social little being full of giggles, smiles, and surprises.

MY BABY GIRL

"The best thing about having a daughter is that you get to be a hero, someone she wishes she was like."

—Tina Marie Martone,
mother of two sons
and one daughter

Three

Watch Her Grow:

Your Daughter from Four to Seven Months

I wish I had taken more pictures of Colleen, during the time she was four to seven months old. In the few frozen moments of time that I have, I see this chubby, little, dimpled face full of smiles. These photos remind me that it doesn't take much to amuse and even enthrall a baby girl through this amazing period of rapid growth.

These months are filled with new adventures. Your daughter is becoming more aware of you and her own role in the world. She is now ready to "talk" to anyone willing to listen, to laugh at funny faces, and giggle with anticipation as you prepare her bath. This is a wonderful time to get to know the little person inside your daughter and smother her with love.

Feeding a Growing Appetite

I had planned to breast-feed Colleen for the entire first year, but she was so little and wasn't gaining as much weight as I hoped. So at about three months, I began to supplement her feedings with formula. At about six months, I offered an occasional teaspoon of baby cereal. The American Academy of Pediatrics wouldn't agree with my decision (it says that most babies need only breast milk or formula for the first six months, or even longer if food allergies run in the family), but to calm hungry babies, many parents introduce solid foods between four and six months, when their child seems ready to handle it.

Although your daughter isn't yet ready for Whopper sandwiches, you might introduce some solid foods after talking to her doctor when you see these signs of readiness:

- ☐ She can sit alone or hold her head up when propped in a sitting position.

- ☐ She can turn her head to avoid something unpleasant.

- ☐ She shows interest in food (she may try to grab your lunch or track each forkful with her eyes as you move it toward your lips).

- ☐ She has lost the tongue-thrust reflex. This reflex leads a newborn to push out foreign matter that enters her mouth. If your daughter still has it, you'll know it after a few tries at feeding because the food that goes in will come right back out. If that happens, you should wait a few weeks and try again.

So your little girl is finally ready for a solid meal! This is a big step, so take it slow. Your daughter's doctor will tell you that you shouldn't make an abrupt switch from bottle or breast milk to solid food. At first, continue to nurse or bottle-feed your daughter while you offer small amounts of solid food only once or twice a day. When babies first start eating solids, they will often eat only a teaspoon or two at a meal. Even after a month or two they may be taking in only three to four tablespoons of food a day, with the rest of their calories coming from breast milk or formula. Most doctors agree that until your daughter approaches her first birthday, solid food will supply some extra calories, but she should get most of her calories and nutrition from breast milk or formula.

FIRST FOODS

Doctors recommend that you introduce solid foods with small amounts of a single food, and offer only that food for several days. Then, you can add new foods one at a time, serving each one a few times before adding the next. This slow introduction will enable you to watch for possible bad reactions and allergies. If the baby gets a rash or diarrhea, for example, after eating one food for two consecutive days, it's easy to tell which food caused it. Once a food has been introduced for three to five days with no problem, you can move onto another.

Typically, the first food offered is a single-grain, iron-fortified baby cereal (usually rice cereal), followed by baby oatmeal or barley cereal. Baby cereals come ready to eat or as dry flakes, to be mixed with breast milk, formula, or water. (Don't mix them with cow's milk until your daughter is a year old.) If you get the ready-to-eat kind, you'll waste a lot of it because your daughter will eat just a little at first and you shouldn't keep the leftovers, even in the refrigerator, for more than a day or two. In either case, you should thin the cereal—in the beginning it should be the consistency of thickened milk.

You can follow up the cereal with pureed fruit (such as banana, peach, apple or pear, but not citrus fruit) or pureed vegetables (especially carrots, peas, squash, sweet potatoes, or green beans). Then you might start giving her pureed meats or chicken. (Some babies seem to dislike meat until they are older. A vegetarian diet for infants is just fine.)

You might introduce finger foods when your daughter has developed enough fine motor control to hold foods and bring them to her mouth, chew (or I should say *gum*), and swallow. This will probably happen sometime between six and seven months. Start out with small cereal pieces (like Cheerios) and let her explore the fun of feeding herself. Wait to introduce finger foods like fruit or hotdogs—right now her ability to chew is not firmly established and these foods pose a choking risk.

BABY FOOD: STORE-BOUGHT OR HOMEMADE?

I made all my own baby food for my first two babies. But by the time Colleen came around, I was so busy that store-bought baby food suddenly looked just fine to me. All three of my children grew healthy and strong, and all three developed their own taste in later years for the commercial, sweetened foods that I had hoped my first two would be spared. So choose whichever is best for your lifestyle regardless of what friends and family say.

Many parents find it's best to use both kinds—buying some baby food for convenience, especially for meals away from home, but making other meals by pureeing or grinding regular food (this is explained a bit later in this chapter). Do whatever makes mealtimes more pleasant for you and your daughter.

Commercial Baby Foods: Commercial baby food is convenient and consistent in taste and nutritional value. It's very safe in terms of being canned without bacterial contamination, and doesn't need refrigeration unless the jars have been opened. Like other processed foods, baby food tends to be lower in pesticide residues than some fresh produce. These days, most baby foods for the youngest children (labeled "Stage 1" foods) are single foods without added salt, sugar, or fillers. Some baby foods even taste pretty good.

If you buy commercial baby food, follow these guidelines:

☐ **Read the labels.** Baby food is formulated for babies of varying ages. Choose ones that match your daughter's age.

☐ **Avoid baby-food desserts.** Your daughter is better off without a lot of added sugar and without coming to expect a sweet finish to every meal. This is one situation when homemade may be better. Serve pureed or mashed fruit, either straight or mixed with a bit of plain yogurt.

☐ **Juices marketed for babies cost more, but most doctors say they aren't necessary.** Your baby's doctor will probably agree that she can drink any 100 percent juice that has been pasteurized.

☐ When you open a jar of baby food for the first time, you should see the center of the lid pop up, as the airtight seal is broken. If it doesn't, don't use the jar.

Homemade Baby Food: If you prefer to make your own baby food, you'll find it is less costly and usually tastier than commercial baby food. If you make it each day, your daughter will get used to the livelier tastes of fresh vegetables and may learn sooner about the pleasures of healthy eating.

However, you should be careful about the fruits and vegetables you choose—when possible, go organic. Regular produce does not have to meet the same standards as produce grown for baby food manufacturers. So if you're not careful, you may end up feeding your daughter more pesticides than if you spooned food from the jar.

If you make your own baby food, follow these guidelines:

☐ If you want to prepare more than one day's worth of food at a time, freeze the extra portions rather than trying to can baby food yourself. (If you freeze pureed food in an ice-cube tray, you can easily pop out one cube at a time.)

☐ Choose raw ingredients and peel or wash them thoroughly.

☐ If you plan to puree or chop processed adult foods, such as canned fruit or frozen vegetables, read the labels to be sure they are not high in salt (sodium), sugar, or other ingredients

BACTERIA ALERT

Whether you use commercial baby food or make your own, place the amount of food you want to use at one feeding in a bowl or food tray and put the rest in the refrigerator in a container with a tight seal. Any food that is not used from that feeding should be thrown away. Do not refrigerate the leftovers; the baby's saliva introduces bacteria into the food, so you should not use it again at another feeding.

you don't want to feed your daughter. Canned soups and canned or jarred pasta with sauce, for example, often contain large amounts of salt.

☐ You can use a blender, food processor, or food mill to chop up food to the proper consistency for babies. Many parents swear by small, plastic food mills that are portable for grinding on the go.

HOW TO FEED YOUR DAUGHTER

It seems that the logical advice here would be: put food on a spoon and place the spoon in your child's mouth. But like so many new adventures with a baby, it's usually not that easy.

We all have to find the best feeding method, but here are some tips that might make it easier for you. In the beginning, nurse or bottle-feed your daughter a little bit before offering her food so she isn't overly hungry. Show her the food and let her touch it, even smear it around if she wants to. Then take a small infant spoon (the rubber-coated kind are gentle in the mouth), a demitasse spoon, or a half-teaspoon from a measuring-spoon set. Put a tiny bit of food on the spoon and place the spoon between her lips. Do not put it far back on her tongue or she may gag.

Once your daughter tastes the food, she may suck it off the spoon and open her mouth for more. She may spit it out but still seem interested. She may gag, cry, or become upset. She may reach for the spoon herself. (Let her play with it. After a while, you can try to guide it to her mouth or you can feed her with another spoon while she hangs on to the first.) As long as your daughter seems interested, you can keep trying. Talk to her in a pleasant tone throughout this process, explaining what you are doing.

After your daughter has had a few spoonfuls or seems tired of the process, finish up the feeding by offering more breast milk or formula. In the beginning, very little food will actually be swallowed, but the goal in the beginning is to teach your daughter to eat, not to meet her nutritional needs with solid food.

FOODS TO AVOID

Some foods are more likely than others to cause allergic or other adverse reactions in babies. Chief among these are cow's milk, eggs, soy, peanuts, and wheat, as well as citrus fruits (including orange juice), shellfish, other nuts, and corn. It is best not to give these to your daughter until she is eating the foods mentioned earlier. If food allergies run in your family, talk to your doctor before giving these foods. Delaying them may reduce the chance of developing allergies. Here are tips on some potential problem foods:

☐ **Cow's milk.** Because its concentrations of protein and minerals are too high for young infants, cow's milk should not be given until a baby is one year old. Even after that age, if you have stopped breast-feeding your daughter she may be better off drinking iron-fortified formula, rather than cow's milk, especially if she is not eating enough iron-rich food, such as meat or iron-fortified cereal. Contrary to what many people think, cow's milk is not essential for a child as long as she gets enough calcium and protein from other sources. Cheese and yogurt are good sources of both. Talk to your daughter's doctor about this.

☐ **Peanuts and peanut butter.** These products can pose a double risk, as a possible cause of allergies and as a choking hazard. (Toddlers and babies can choke on sticky globs of peanut butter as well as on the nuts themselves.) To be safest on both counts, wait until age three before giving peanut butter, and even then spread it on bread or crackers, rather than serving it plain. Wait until age four to serve nuts.

☐ **Honey and corn syrup.** Do not give these sweeteners to children who are less than a year old. They can contain bacterial spores that may cause botulism (a serious illness) in babies, but not in older children or adults.

A NOTE ON NEATNESS

Learning to eat can be a messy process—and likely to get much messier as your daughter gets older and starts feeding herself. For the next few years, much of your daughter's meal may well end up on the floor. You can try to save yourself cleanup time by putting a small plastic drop cloth under her chair, but then you have to clean the plastic. Instead, put old newspaper under the chair that you can throw out afterwards, or put down a fabric tablecloth that you can shake out and throw in the washing machine.

Bibs are a must! They come in all shapes and sizes, but whatever you choose, use one at every meal to save yourself the trouble of having to give your daughter a complete change of clothes after eating. Plastic bibs are nice because they can be sponged off, and the rigid plastic kind—which look a bit like a knight's breast plate—have a pocket at the bottom that catches dropped morsels. Be sure to take the bib off your daughter in between meals to avoid the risk of choking or strangulation, and be particularly careful with bibs that tie on with strings.

Fashion for Little Girls

Obviously, baby fashions have not caught on to the concept of gender equality. Baby girls still wear the pink frills and bows so popular in their mother's and grandmother's day. For what is probably a complex collection of reasons, our society wants to see little girls in pink. However, I've often suspected that parents buy pink, "feminine" clothing for their little girls because that's all they can find in the stores. We don't really have a choice about continuing the "pink is for girls and blue is for boys" mind-set if clothing designers offer no options. Right?

Well, not exactly, according to Freddie Curtis, director of the fashion design and fashion merchandising programs at Harcum College in Bryn Mawr Pennsylvania. Curtis knows firsthand what fashions sell for little girls and what don't because she makes baby blankets and sweaters that are sold in upscale boutiques in large metropolitan areas such as Philadelphia, Washington D.C., New York, Miami, and Houston. Curtis has found that no matter how sophisticated or educated parents may be, they still want to dress their little girls in pink. She says that although she'd like to offer a wider variety of colors, people don't buy them. In fact, Curtis says that every time she uses a blue floral print or even a soft blue plaid for her little girl's line, she gets stuck with it because nobody wants to put a baby girl in blue, even if it's floral or pastel. "Once in a while a store will buy items in gender-neutral colors," she says, "but very rarely do they sell well."

As infants grow into little girls, parents do have a bit more flexibility in their fashion choices (and in the way they think about gender identity) than parents of little boys. Curtis points out that although parents will *never* dress their sons in pink, some will put their daughters in blue clothing—usually with a pink flower embroidered on it somewhere.

It's an interesting cultural phenomenon that we've decided somewhere along the line to associate pink only with girls—and we're not ready to budge from that conviction. So for now, the stores stay fully stocked with pink dresses with lace and bows for little girls. The truth, however, is that your daughter could care less what color or style her clothes are. And wearing or not wearing pink won't change the way she views herself as a female as she grows up.

Grandparents, Dolls, and Pink Dresses

Having loving grandparents is a blessing for all children. The importance of this relationship is supported by reams of research showing that children with the support of loving grandparents have a greater sense of family and self-worth. I have always believed that there can never be too many loving adults in a child's life. But sometimes it has been hard to remember this.

My mother-in-law had two sons and no daughters. So when my Colleen was born, my mother-in-law was beaming. She couldn't wait to buy her all the little-girl clothes and toys, ribbons, and bows in the world. She also wanted to spend a lot of time with her new granddaughter. That was a problem for me. This new grandma believed that it was her divine right (and even duty!) to spoil her granddaughter in every way possible. She did not care that sweets before dinner would ruin a little girl's appetite. It didn't matter if playing in mud would destroy good clothes. As long as Colleen was happy, that's all that mattered. When Grandma got the chance to spend a few hours alone with her granddaughter, she would nod and smile as I gave her my list of dos and don'ts, and then thoroughly enjoy spoiling her by breaking every rule I set. We had many disagreements over our different views of child rearing—that I now regret.

My mother-in-law died recently and my children (and I) miss her terribly. I now realize that the love she gave my daughter was far more important and valuable than the fact that the way she chose to give it was different from my own. I should have found a better way to compromise and balance her parenting style with my own.

One area that often needs rather heavy-handed balancing is the issue of gender stereotypes in toys and clothing. Thanks to the feminist movement in the 1970s, today's grandparents are far more aware of unnecessary gender stereotypes than in generations past. But when it comes to their own grandchildren, you may find that your parents and in-laws have some views that differ from your own.

Maureen O'Brien, Ph.D., director of parenting and child development at The First Years, Inc., in Avon, Massachusetts and author of *Watch Me Grow: I'm One-Two-Three* says that from birth to age two, a baby is learning who she is as a person and what it means to be a girl. As a developmental psychologist, she points out that any adult who spends a good amount of time with your daughter will influence her development.

"Your daughter's grandparents come into the picture with a whole set of expectations: what they think babies should be like, what kind of activities they should be involved in, what kind of personality is 'appropriate' for the gender of the baby," O'Brien observes. "They might also bring their own dashed expectations from when they were parents: maybe they wanted a daughter but had only boys, maybe they wanted a daughter who would play dress up, but got a tree climber instead. Like parents, grandparents bring a whole lifetime of experience to their relationship with the baby. This can be wonderful if those expectations are in line with what you want your child to be exposed to, but it can be quite a challenge if you don't agree."

O'Brien feels that during infancy is a good time to hash out this difference of opinion because your daughter isn't yet aware of the push-pull that may go on between you and your own parents. But by toddlerhood, she will be very much aware of any differences you have. This is the time to explain yourself if you have strong feelings about the kinds of toys and clothing that grandparents should give to your daughter, or the kinds of play activities that are or are not appropriate.

For example, some parents feel strongly that fairy tales are very sexist and stereotypical. Your daughter won't notice this yet, but if these are the kind of stories she hears from infancy on, by the time she is three or four years old she will pick up the stereotypes and will act out the part. Your daughter will see herself as the helpless damsel in distress, and she will see boys as the heroes, the conquerors, and the saviors. When grandparents insist on reading and rereading these tales to babies, a battle often erupts. The fight may be a worthy one, but O'Brien believes it's probably a losing one.

"If you want to bring up your child in a gender-neutral world," she says, "the reality is you don't have a chance because the world is not gender-neutral. You have to be realistic and realize that there is a whole world of influence that will show your children gender stereotypes." In fact, O'Brien says that by themselves these stereotypes are not necessarily a bad thing. In their neutral form, they are just another way to categorize things. When kids are first starting to learn about the world, they do it in many ways: big things, little things; loud things, quiet things; girl things, boy things. It is a helpful way for them to put order in their world. Labeling is natural and harmless. It's when a category becomes biased that it can become troublesome. Girls are dainty and therefore helpless; boys are brave and therefore never cry. We contribute to this kind of gender bias when we scold our little boys for trying on Mommy's shoes or tell our daughters that they can't help Daddy with the yard work because girls shouldn't get dirty.

So if your daughter's grandparents are stuck on gender stereotypes and buy her only pink and frilly clothing and fairy-tale books, they're not going to create a problem that isn't in the world at large and that will touch your child eventually anyway.

O'Brien saw this in her own family. "I gave my baby boys plenty of dolls," she says, "but as they grew into the grade school years, they tossed them aside and spent more time with trucks. I can't blame myself or anyone else for that. But now that they're ten years old I do notice that they have less stereotypical ideas than boys of my generation. When I talk about a doctor, for example, they will ask, 'Is it a boy or a girl doctor?' The fact that they can ask that question shows me that my efforts have given them some degree of gender respect, and that, after all, was my goal."

If Grandma and Grandpa have stereotypical ideas and argue that you should throw away your daughter's construction set and buy her a doll, you don't have to let this difference of opinion escalate into a major battle. When they arrive with one more doll or pink dress, just say thanks with a smile and add it to the pile. When the grandparents leave, you can offer your daughter a balanced experience with gender-neutral toys as well.

You'll find that as your daughter grows she will be exposed to many things you don't like but can't control. Your goal in all these situations should be to make your home the place where she learns she is valued and loved as a person regardless of the toys she plays with or the style of clothes she wears.

Sweet Dreams

We all have a biological clock that governs our sleep-wake cycles, making us sleepy at certain times and wakeful at others. Our sleep-wake clock is "set" each day by darkness and light, especially exposure to bright morning light. Newborns do not have this biological rhythm and will wake and sleep around the clock regardless of daylight or nightfall. Then, usually by three months of age, they develop an internal sleep-wake clock.

You can help your daughter set her internal clock to better match your own simply by putting her to bed and waking her at the same time every day. A consistent waking time seems to be especially important to setting this clock and forming good sleep patterns.

Some babies develop regular sleep-wake patterns as early as six or eight weeks, but usually these patterns emerge around three or four months. At that age, most babies average three to five hours of sleep during the day, usually grouped into two or three naps, and ten to twelve hours at night, usually with an interruption or two for feeding.

It wasn't long before I discovered what the phrase *sleep through the night* really means. It is defined as sleeping five hours in a row. So if I put my babies down at 9 P.M., and they were up again at 2 A.M., they had slept "through the night" and I didn't even know it! With this in mind, it's probably best to put your daughter down for the night as close to midnight as possible.

HOW TO HELP YOUR DAUGHTER FALL ASLEEP

It may seem unnecessary to teach a baby how to fall asleep—most do a pretty good job of that without any lessons. But if your daughter is six months old and still calling for you in the middle of the night, she needs to learn how to fall asleep *by herself*. If you always rock, feed, or soothe her to sleep, you take away her natural ability to self-soothe and therefore cause her to be more dependent on you.

I was the world's worst offender in this department. I had unknowingly taught my son Joey to connect my presence with falling asleep. Then, if I was not able (or willing) to always rock or feed him back to sleep, he would cry through the night. This middle child was two years old before he finally slept from nighttime to daybreak. That blessed event happened only after I took him to a crying-baby clinic I saw advertised in the newspaper. I was at my wits' end and would do anything to make this child sleep by himself.

At the clinic I met Charles Schaefer, Ph.D., who offered me a plan. His method actually worked, and eventually I helped him write the book *Teach Your Baby to Sleep Through the Night*. Here are the basics:

1. Say goodnight. When you put your daughter to bed for the night, say goodnight and leave the bedroom *before* your child is asleep. Keep reminding yourself that your daughter is capable of falling asleep on her own without your help. You just have to teach her how.

The bedroom should be exactly the same when you first say

goodnight as it will be when your daughter wakes up in the middle of the night: no overhead light, no music, no parent.

2. Wait. If your daughter cries when you leave at bedtime or awakens crying at night, wait five minutes before responding.

3. Check. Make a quick check on her to reassure yourself that she is all right. This quick check should be just that—quick. Stay with your daughter only one or two minutes to clean up any mess or to make sure she is not feverish, in pain, too hot, or too cold. Do not pick her up. Rather:

- ☐ Get up close to her.

- ☐ Establish eye contact.

- ☐ Maintain a neutral facial expression.

- ☐ Use a firm voice to say her name and give a simple, direct command such as, "Go to sleep."

- ☐ Do not scream, become hostile, or hit her.

- ☐ Do not sympathize, hug, or show your own distress.

4. Check again. If the crying persists for another twenty minutes after the first check, go again to check on your daughter and remind her that you expect sleep, not crying, at this hour. Do not feed, rock, or pick her up. Leave again before she is asleep.

Repeat this procedure of briefly checking on your daughter after every twenty-minute crying spell for as long as it takes her to finally get tired and fall asleep. If she is crying softly or whimpering at the end of a twenty-minute period, do not go and check because she is probably close to falling asleep on her own.

Twenty minutes seems to be optimal length of time to let infant night-wakers cry. On many occasions, they will fall back to sleep on their own after ten to fifteen minutes.

5. Stick to the daily schedule. Awaken your daughter at her usual time in the morning. Do not allow her to sleep any later regardless of how little sleep you or she had the night before. Also, keep her daily nap schedule intact. Do not allow her to take more or longer naps during the day. As tempting as it will be to make up for lost sleep during the day, try to resist. Doing so will disturb the wake-sleep rhythms you're trying to develop to ensure a good night's sleep.

Dr. Schaefer expected that this routine would teach my son to put himself to sleep within three nights. It took a grueling five, but it was worth it! I had had two years of being sleep deprived, exhausted, and irritable. It was time to do something about it. Besides, (I kept reminding myself), Dr. Schaefer said that a baby's learning to calm herself can be a step in a little girl's long path to independence, fostering a sense of competence and self-confidence. As long it occurs in the context of a close, loving relationship, it causes no emotional damage.

If after trying this method for one week (without giving in occasionally), your six-month-old continues to wake up several times each night and cry for your attention, talk to your pediatrician about it. There may be something else bothering her.

Child-Proofing Your Home

People without young children must have thought I had the worst sense of interior design on the planet. When my children were babies, my house looked like I just moved in and hadn't yet put out the knickknacks, plants, and other decorative touches that make a house a home. But I learned very quickly that it was far better for all of us if breakables were packed away, sharp objects were moved to higher ground, and cabinets and drawers were locked tight.

I also learned that it's never "too soon" to start child-proofing. While your daughter is between four and seven months, take a good look around your home and begin to think about safety. Because you can't predict the day she'll learn to roll over to the electrical cord, or scoot on her behind to the edge of the stairs, or eventually crawl across the room to the hot stove, take time now to prevent accidents and injuries by making a few simple changes in your household. Here's a list to get you started:

☐ Survey your house for hazards, then search again. Walk slowly through the house looking for potential danger. Then, crawl through the house to get a baby's perspective.

☐ Move all sharp objects, including knives, forks, vegetable peelers, and sewing or hobby implements out of reach or get latches and locks for drawers and cabinets. Drawer latches of various designs are widely available through stores, catalogs, and websites that sell baby products.

☐ Move anything that could be swallowed into high or locked cabinets or closets. This includes medicines, vitamins, cleansers, cosmetics, detergents, stain removers, air fresheners, candles, and pet food. Regular human food can also choke a baby and should not be easily accessible.

☐ If you have drawers that can be pulled out all the way without stopping, install latches or stops so your daughter doesn't pull them out onto herself.

☐ Put outlet covers on or plugs in unused electric sockets.

☐ Check for hanging wires, blind cords, and similar objects that could be pulled down or could choke a baby.

☐ Move any objects that could break or fall.

☐ Move high-risk furniture or make it safe. Tall bookcases and dressers should be secured to the walls with brackets, so that if a child climbs on them they won't tumble over on top of her. You can buy elasticized padding to put around the hard edges of tables that might be in a toddler's path.

☐ Be prepared to install gates to block off staircases. (Use the kind that mounts to the wall with hardware.)

You won't catch all potential hazards (and so you should never leave your daughter "loose" and unsupervised). But this list should prevent the most obvious dangers. You should repeat this process every time your daughter moves up in mobility—when she starts to crawl, walk, run, and climb.

FIVE SAFETY ITEMS
YOUR HOME SHOULD HAVE

To safeguard your daughter in times of emergency, stock up on these five safety items:

- smoke detectors
- fire extinguishers
- carbon monoxide detector
- flashlights
- escape ladder

CHECK FOR LEAD PAINT

Lead paint was banned in 1978 because it was found to cause lead poisoning. But if your home was built before that date, you should have painted areas, both exterior and interior, checked by the local department of health to see if your child is in danger of lead paint exposure.

Lead paint is seductively sweet. If young children eat paint chips or inhale lead dust, they can suffer lead poisoning. Milder forms of lead poisoning have been associated with learning problems, and severe cases can cause mental retardation and many physical problems. If lead paint is found in your home, ideally it should be removed or covered with paneling or plasterboard before your daughter arrives. (Lead paint is best removed by professionals who know how to contain the lead dust it produces.) It is also important to identify areas coated with lead paint if you plan to renovate rooms because such work can create and spread lead dust.

If you are a renter and your landlord refuses to have your apartment checked for lead, contact your local health department. Rules about if and when landlords can be required to remove or cover over lead paint vary from place to place. If your landlord resists following the rules, you may need to seek help from the health department, tenants' groups, or health advocacy groups.

Medical Care

The four- to seven-month-old baby girl is a medical marvel. The healthy infant kicks, rocks, and rolls with vigor and gusto during all waking hours. But when she's not feeling well, she can't tell you about it, so you'll have to notice the change in feeding and activity level, which will tip you off. Sometimes you can handle the problem yourself. Other times you'll need to call your daughter's doctor. The information in this section will help you distinguish between normal childhood discomforts (like teething and overheating) and those that require a professional's care.

ROUTINE AT-HOME HEALTH CARE

You work hard every day to keep your little girl comfortable and happy. You change her diaper before her bottom gets red; you feed her tummy before she screams from hunger pains; you rock her, sing to her, and hold her close. Here are some pointers about keeping that comfort level high as the seasons change and also as the pain of teething begins.

Seasonal Care: Fresh air and a change of surroundings are good for you and your daughter, so take her out for walks if the weather is nice. Just be careful to dress her properly—not too much and not too little.

An infant's body loses heat more readily than an older child's or adult's. This makes it difficult for her body to regulate temperature when she's exposed to excessive heat or cold during the first year or so of life. In general, she should wear one more layer (of clothing or a blanket) than you do when it is cold.

If it is uncomfortably cold, keep your daughter inside if possible. If you have to go out, dress her in warm sweaters or put bunting bags over her other clothes, and place a warm hat over her head and ears. You can shield her face from the cold with a blanket when she's outside, but hold it far enough from her nose and mouth so she can breathe easily.

To check whether your daughter is clothed warmly enough, feel her hands and feet and the skin on her chest. Her hands and feet should be slightly cooler than her body but not cold. Her chest should feel warm. If her hands, feet, and chest feel cold, take her into a warm room, unwrap her, and hold her close so the heat from your body warms her.

In warm or hot weather, you can ease up on the layers. Dress your daughter as you dress yourself to feel comfortable—and, of course, protecting her from direct sun rays.

Babies less than six months old should be kept out of direct sun entirely because they are prone to sunburn and heatstroke, both of which can be dangerous at this age. Keep them in the shade of a tree, umbrella, or stroller canopy. For years, the American Academy of Pediatrics recommended against putting sunblock on babies under six months because of concerns about the way their skin might absorb the chemicals. But in 1999, the Academy changed its position, saying that if clothing and shade to block the sun are not available, it may be reasonable to apply sunscreen to small areas, such as the face and back of the hands. Still, the best way to protect your daughter from the sun's ultraviolet rays is to keep her out of the sun.

Teething: Although it's not time to bring on the steak, your daughter will probably cut her first teeth during this infant period. By the time babies are born, they have a full set of primary teeth (commonly called baby teeth) hidden below the gum line, as well as the beginnings of the permanent teeth that will come later. The first

TEETHING TIMELINE

Five to six months: Teething begins. The first tooth to appear is usually one in the bottom front. Because teeth appear in pairs, the second tooth (the mate to the lower incisor) will appear often within days of the first.

About eight months: The two upper front teeth will emerge.

By twelve months: The four incisors (on each side of the front teeth) appear and the first molars begin to emerge.

All twenty primary teeth—ten on top, ten on the bottom—are usually in by age three.

baby tooth usually breaks through when your daughter is between four and seven months, although the big event may occur as early as three months or as late as twelve months.

Your daughter will let you know when she's teething. There's no mistaking the drool that will run down her chin all day long. She also is likely to chew on anything she can get her hands on, to ease the discomfort. Some babies have short bursts of irritability, while some may seem cranky for weeks, crying frequently, waking more often, and eating fretfully. For others, the process seems to be almost completely painless. As the gums grow tender and swollen, her body temperature may be a little higher than normal, but as a rule, teething does not cause high fever, diarrhea, earaches, runny noses, or coughing (as some well-intentioned friends and relatives may tell you).

To make teething more pleasant for your daughter try these simple teething strategies:

☐ Wipe your daughter's face often with a soft cloth to remove the drool and prevent rashes or irritation.

☐ Place a clean, flat cloth (such as a diaper not used for diapering) under her head when you lay her down to sleep. If she drools, you can replace it with a dry cloth without having to change the whole sheet.

☐ Try rubbing your daughter's gums with a clean finger. (Do not coat your finger with sugar or honey.)

☐ Give your daughter something firm to chew on, but be sure it's not small enough to swallow and can't break into pieces that might pose a choking risk. (Bagels, which are used as teething rings by some parents, are not a good choice for this reason. Neither are teething biscuits, despite their name, or frozen bananas.) Hard rubber teething rings can be good; look for one-piece models.

☐ Make it cold. Many babies seem to enjoy teething on objects that have been chilled but aren't rock-hard. Try freezing a clean wet washcloth for thirty minutes, then let your daughter chew on it.

☐ If your daughter seems to be in a lot of pain, it may be worth giving her acetaminophen drops, but consult her doctor first. Ditto for painkillers that are applied to the gums (such as Baby Orajel or Baby Anbesol). These provide relief for a short time that may be just long enough to let her fall asleep.

☐ Never use old home remedies such as placing an aspirin against the gum or rubbing the gum with any type of alcohol. And don't clean those little teeth with a fluoride toothpaste. She may swallow some paste, which can result in tooth staining or surface irregularities on the enamel.

ROUTINE MEDICAL CHECKUP

Lots of adults do not arrange for periodic routine medical checkups for themselves as they should. We put them off and plan to keep the appointment next year—hopefully with no major harm done. But when it comes to our babies, there's no putting it off. Infants need regular checkups on a rather strict schedule so that their doctor can monitor their medical and developmental progress, give required inoculations, and catch any problems early on.

I never missed an infant checkup with my kids, but I can't say that I really knew why they were so important. So I've again asked Stephen Muething, M.D. at Cincinnati Children's Hospital Medical Center to tell us what happens at these checkups that most physicians will schedule for your daughter at four and six months of age.

Dr. Muething says the physician will give your daughter a thorough physical as he did in previous visits. Again he will weigh and measure her (see the growth chart information in Appendix A for expected measurements), and then measure her head (a baby's head will grow about one-half inch every month for the first six months). He will listen to your daughter's heart and lungs with a stethoscope. He will examine her legs, feet, and overall skin color and condition, as well as her genital area. Finally, he will examine your daughter's eyes, nose, ears, and throat for signs of good health.

Your daughter will probably be given immunizations at one or both of these visits. The typical infant gets twelve immunization shots within the first six months. This is far more than your parents may remember. These shots protect children against hepatitis B, polio, measles, mumps, rubella (German measles), pertussis (whooping cough), diphtheria, tetanus (lockjaw), Haemophilus influenza type b, pneumococcal infections, and chickenpox. Be sure to follow your doctor's instructions on when these inoculations are due. The recommended schedule does change from time to time, but you can find the most up-to-date recommended immunization schedule on the website of the American Academy of Pediatrics at www.aap.org, or the Centers For Disease Control at www.cdc.gov/nip/acip.

The four- and six-month visits are also the time when your daughter's doctor will want to hear about her feeding schedules. Many moms who started nursing will now be adding some formula or switching entirely to formula. During this period, many parents introduce some kind of solid foods. The doctor will discuss your daughter's feedings and offer some advice on how to continue to introduce new foods and watch for possible bad reactions.

Sleep is another subject that often concerns parents when babies are between four and seven months. "Some parents come in," says Dr. Muething, "with that look of fatigue, and I know that sleep is an issue we need to talk about." If your daughter is not yet sleeping through the night, now is the time to talk about that.

After the basics are covered, Dr. Muething notes that parents should be prepared to ask any questions they have. "After the first few visits where parents are concerned about the baby's physical health," he says, "they now start to focus on the baby's development. They want to make sure their daughter is doing what she's supposed to be doing at the right time. Is she developing physically and intellectually as she should be? Most often, moms know something is wrong before the doctor says anything. They know it in their heart, but don't want to say it." These routine checkups give you an opportunity to make sure your daughter is progressing as she should:

☐ At four to six months, she should be able to sit with some support. She may also be able to roll over from her back to her side and from stomach to back.

☐ Your daughter should now have some hand-eye coordination and be able to grab at things she sees. She grabs at objects and brings her hands or the objects close to her face to her mouth. She also opens and closes her hands so that she can pick up and look at objects.

☐ All babies this age should begin to be social, and be able to track visually, interact with parents, smile responsively, coo, and make noise.

WHEN TO CALL THE DOCTOR

If your daughter has symptoms of a cold, fever, or flu you may wonder if you should call the doctor. Dr. Meuthing says, "The way the baby is feeding is important when deciding whether or not to call the doctor. If the baby is feeding well, then we're not that concerned. But if she is not feeding well, or has stopped feeding completely, we want the parents to call. A baby's number-one job is to eat and grow. If she can't get the job done, something is wrong and we should check it out."

When you call the doctor because your daughter seems ill, it helps to be specific and focused, especially if you are not calling during office hours.

☐ Remind the doctor of your child's age, past and continuing medical problems (including low birth weight or prematurity), and any medications, including over-the-counter drugs or supplements that she is taking.

☐ Describe the symptoms that led you to call. Say when the symptoms started, how they have changed, and how you have handled them so far. Be as specific as possible: "She usually wakes up to eat every four hours, but we've had to wake her for the last three feedings" is a description that tells the doctor more than if you just say your daughter is unusually sleepy.

☐ Spell out what you are concerned about: "Her cough seems to be getting worse, and now that it's bedtime I'm worried she'll have trouble breathing during the night."

☐ Mention all the symptoms that concern you, but don't mix in routine issues that could be dealt with some other time, such as whether to use a pacifier or when to start solid food.

☐ Take your daughter's temperature before you call and write it down, along with the time it was taken.

☐ If your daughter has vomited or has diarrhea, be prepared to describe when, how often, and what it looked like.

☐ Try to notice whether your daughter is urinating as much as usual. If not, be sure to tell the doctor.

☐ Have a pad at hand to write down instructions. Have your daughter's health record available to update and give additional information if necessary.

☐ Have the name and number of your pharmacy available in case the doctor wants to call in a prescription.

COMMON HEALTH CONCERNS

As your daughter spends less time in your protective arms and more time on the floor exploring her world, there's more to think about to keep her safe and healthy. A good child-proofing plan as explained earlier should protect her from most harmful situations, but babies have a way of finding trouble even in the most guarded homes. Here are some tips you should keep in mind as your daughter reaches out to examine her world.

Preventing Choking: As your daughter begins to get around by rolling and scooting across the floor, she's bound to find interesting things to put in her mouth. A dropped coin or a forgotten watch battery is irresistible to your little explorer. But they are also choking hazards.

If your daughter's airway becomes blocked, she will not be able to breathe or make normal sounds and her face will turn from bright red to blue. If your daughter is coughing but is still able to breathe and make noises, the airway is not fully blocked, and she will likely clear the airway by herself by coughing it up. Don't attempt to remove an object by trying to reach in and grasping it with your fingers. That could push it farther into her throat and totally block the airway. Instead, let the child cough to expel the object herself.

If your daughter is choking, conscious but cannot breathe, and is turning blue, the situation requires immediate intervention. The first step is to call 911. While you wait for professional help, you can administer the modified Heimlich maneuver that is recommended for infants under age one. Because the infant's organs are

CAR SEAT SAFETY

Once your daughter reaches twenty pounds or twenty-six inches and can sit up by herself, you can move her to a forward-facing car seat, but still keep her in the back seat. Front-passenger air bags can kill a child when they deploy. If you have any questions about moving from a rear-facing to a forward-facing seat, call the Federal Auto Safety Hotline at 800-424-9393.

fragile, the regular Heimlich that you may already know cannot be used. In this situation, you can't learn the modified version on the spot by reading from a book while you're panicked about your choking baby (and I'm not brave enough to try to teach it to you through the printed word). Plan ahead. Ask your daughter's doctor to show you how the modified Heimlich works. Practice it over and over so that if you should face an emergency choking situation, you'll know exactly what to do.

Physical Growth

Your daughter will double her birth weight by the time she is four to six months old and she will grow about one to one and a half inches each month. Overall, your daughter is beginning to look less like an infant and more like a person with her own distinctive appearance (a once-bald head may now be showing a bit of hair).

By sixteen to twenty weeks, most infants can turn their heads to both sides, and between twenty-four and twenty-eight weeks they'll lift their heads while lying on their backs. Between six and seven months, you'll notice that the muscles in your daughter's arms and legs are growing quite sturdy (the better to soon scoot all around your house with!). Her body proportions are changing as her lower body becomes bigger and stronger. This will allow her to start rolling from one place to another between eight and ten weeks, and then somewhere between six and nine months to creep on her stomach and drag her legs behind.

PREMATURE BABY GIRLS

If your daughter was born very premature, her gender may give her a growth advantage. A 2003 study out of Children's Hospital in Ohio found that girls born about ten weeks early weighing less than three pounds were more likely than premature boys to catch up with their peers in growth by age twenty. It's thought that the effects of female hormones that kick in when girls reach puberty may partly explain their catch-up growth. This same study also found that the premature boys were generally sicker babies than the premature girls, echoing previous research.

FINE MOTOR SKILL DEVELOPMENT

As your daughter's large muscles are developing to prepare her for action, her fine motor skills are also maturing so that she can better hold, handle, and manipulate things in her world.

By six months, most infants can briefly hold on to an object like a small block and will soon learn to bang two blocks together. You'll also see that, although the way she grasps things is a bit clumsy, she is fascinated by this ability. In fact, she'll try to grab anything in her sight—even pictures in a book.

By seven months, you'll see that she can not only grab and hold an object, but let go of it, too. I remember the look of absolute joy when my daughter discovered that she could pick up her food, release her grasp, and drop it on the floor. It was a skill she practiced over and over again! At this time, your daughter can also move the object from one hand to another. So keep a few blocks on hand for her to grab and manipulate, place them just within her reach, and watch her fine motor skills grow.

Emotional Development

While your daughter is growing larger in size and physical capabilities, she is also growing emotionally. She is learning about feelings such as accomplishment and security, and she's starting to recognize that she is a separate human being who is very special.

EXPLORING WHO I AM

Although it's hard to imagine, your daughter has no idea that you and she are not one and the same person. In fact, babies have no way of knowing that any other people exist separately from themselves at all. A sense of self as a separate body and mind, distinct from others, does not develop until the child is about eighteen months old. Much of life before this time is devoted to learning to make this distinction.

This self-awareness begins with a thorough exploration of the body. What a joy to watch a baby this age examine her hands and feet. She stares and studies them for long periods, memorizing what they look like and how they work. I imagine she is saying to herself, "What a piece of work I am!"

Your daughter's increasing ability to control her body movements also contributes to her growing sense of self. As she comes to realize that she can manipulate and interact with her world (by taking off her socks for example), she gains strong feelings of mastery and accomplishment. Each success contributes to her view of who she is and her value in the universe.

DEALING WITH FEAR AND FRUSTRATION

Being an infant in an ever-changing world is not always easy. Your daughter may start to show signs of fear and frustration as she tries to understand her world and often falls short.

Babies develop fears about the most ordinary things. Your daughter may one day panic when you remove her clothes and she feels discomfort about being naked. Or she may throw a fit when you try to lower her into a warm water bath. Or, she may suddenly become afraid of her stuffed animal. These fears are usually short-lived and nothing to worry about. They are signs that your little girl is becoming more aware of her environment and the fact that not all of it makes sense to her.

You can help your daughter get past these fears by accepting them and working to help her deal with them. If, for example, she doesn't like to be naked, keep a light blanket nearby that you can gently put over her, even when you're changing her clothes. If she doesn't want to take a bath, sponge bathe her for a while. If she screams every time she see a certain toy, put the toy away. Don't worry about "babying" her and feeding her fears. She *is* a baby, and right now she needs to know that you respect her feelings and are there to protect her.

This is also a time when your baby girl will get frustrated when she can't do all the things she wants to do. If she wants a toy that's just out of reach, she may now scream at her failed attempt to grab it. If she wants the bottle that's sitting on the counter but can't get it herself, she'll let out a howl—not of hunger as she would earlier—but of frustration.

When this happens, it's sometimes best to stand back and watch for a little bit rather than jump to the rescue. If, for example, your daughter is trying to get a block out of a box, but finds that it's stuck, don't help her right away. Give her a chance to work it out, to try harder, to accomplish the task herself. By not running to the rescue too quickly, you teach your daughter how to handle the frustration that often comes when she is learning something new. She'll eventually learn that if she keeps trying she'll be successful. This is far better than learning to look to you solve all her problems.

Cognitive Development

Your daughter is polishing up her thinking skills every time she touches, smells, sees, feels, and tastes her world. Between four and seven months, you'll start to see evidence of all that she's been learning.

WHAT YOUR BABY GIRL KNOWS

Watch your daughter closely as she examines a toy and you can almost picture the wheels in her head turning. You can see her thinking, "If I do this, then that will happen." You can see this cause-and-effect thinking process when she intentionally kicks at an object to make it move. She will slam her open hand on a toy to make it squeak. And she'll even drop her bottle on the floor just for the joy of knowing that you'll retrieve it.

Anticipation is an advanced thinking skill for a little one. You'll see this intellectual feat when you wiggle your finger and move in slowly to tickle her tummy. After playing this game a few times she learns to anticipate the tickle and will squeal with delight before your finger touches her body. You'll also see signs of this skill when she smiles and waves her arms and legs as you begin to prepare her bath. She knows the chance for some good splashing is on its way.

This is also time for some major experimentation. Your daughter is starting to be interested in how things work and what they do. Watch as she pokes at a toy, bangs another, and shakes a third. She's experimenting to find out which ones roll, which ones make noise, and which ones do nothing at all. Around six to seven months, she'll start to remember how things work and she'll know in advance that the rattle will make noise and that slapping her hand on her bath water will make a wonderful splash.

You can help your daughter in her quest to learn all about her world. Because she learns so much by simply watching, give her a change of view every so often. Move her to different places around the room and the house so she can see different perspectives. Take her outside, bring her to the park, take a walk with her stroller. These experiences are all learning opportunities.

You can also use your simple daily activities as teaching tools. Here are a few to get you started:

☐ Explain what you're doing as you put the key in the lock to open the door. Point out that the water from the tap can fill up the container.

☐ Place your daughter's toy under the blanket and ask, "Where is it?" She'll eventually learn to look for it and will be delighted by her mastery of this fascinating game.

☐ When you hear a family member approaching, ask, "Who is coming?" When the person arrives, name him or her so your daughter learns both to anticipate and to name.

LANGUAGE DEVELOPMENT: *MAMA!*

Although your daughter won't be talking for a while yet, she's learning a lot about language. Her ability to understand words will be far greater than her speaking vocabulary, so don't assume that because your daughter isn't talking yet, there's no point in talking to her. During these few months, you'll notice that she will respond to certain familiar words. If you ask her where the dog is, she'll look around for it. If you call her name, she will turn to you. If you ask her where Daddy is, she'll look right at him. There's lots of language development going on before your daughter says her first word.

Between four and five months your daughter may make her first attempts to communicate by making the most delightful sound—I call it razzing. She'll blow through her lips, often with saliva bubbles, to make a vibrating sound and then laugh at her accomplishment. If you razz her right back, she's likely to keep the game going.

Around six months, she'll begin to imitate one-syllable sounds. This is when you'll swear that your daughter called your name: *ma* or *da*. Soon she will put together two syllables and you'll hear (over and over) her favorite sounds such as *mama, dada,* and *baba,* as well as repetitive syllables such as *a-la-la.*

This is also the time when your daughter is learning what words mean. By seven months she will begin to understand specific words that she hears often, such as *bottle* or *blanket.* The way you talk to your daughter will directly affect how well her language skills develop. In fact, the more often you have "conversations" with your daughter, the more developed the language center of her brain will become. Try these strategies to improve your daughter's language skills:

☐ **Talk to her.** As you rush through your day, talk out loud and tell your daughter what you're doing. As you put on her shoes, say something like, *Shoes go on your feet.* Even if the words you say mean nothing to your daughter, she's learning the sound, pitch, inflection, and rhythm of language.

☐ **Talk back.** When your daughter makes a sound, keep the conversation going. Look at her and mimic the sound back. Let her know you're listening to her and enjoy her attempts at communication.

☐ **Use precise words to label objects.** Instead of using the general word *toy*, use the specific word such as *ball* or *rattle*.

☐ **Match your tone of voice to your meaning.** If you use a soft, singsong voice to tell your daughter *Don't touch that,* it will be hard for her to understand what you mean. If you are giving a warning, she needs to hear a firm tone that matches the message.

☐ **Be silly.** Don't worry that your daughter will pick up bad speech habits if you occasionally use baby talk, singsong words, or even silly, nonsense syllables.

At this age, the most important thing is to enjoy the give and take of communication. Make it fun for your daughter to listen and learn.

ENJOYING A GOOD BOOK

You don't have to wait until your little girl is older to read her a bedtime story. Even infants love a good book. The all-time favorite in my house was *Pat the Bunny*. My babies loved it because each turn of the page gave them a new texture to feel. They would bang their little hands against the cardboard page and delight in the feel of the soft fur, and then more gently touch the scratchy paper.

While you read to your daughter, for a short while she will carefully listen to the cadences of your words and phrases with rapt attention. She is learning to speak by listening to your voice as its tone, pitch, and inflection changes.

Reading picture books to your daughter also helps her learn about her world. She will enjoy looking at books with pictures of things she finds in her own world: babies, toys, familiar animals, and vehicles. As you show her these pictures, name them and when appropriate, make accompanying sounds. If you have a cat in your home, for example, get a picture book about a cat, and as you read it to your daughter, point to the picture and then to your family cat, name the animal—"cat"—and add a meow. There's so much to learn and books are a great way to make that learning fun—even for infants.

BABY GAMES

Play is the occupation of children. It is what allows them to grow intellectually as they learn to problem-solve (when figuring out where the teddy bear is hiding), to manipulate (when putting a toy held in one hand into the other hand), to learn cause and effect (when pushing a button makes the music play), and so on. So don't wait for your daughter to be up and running around and making her own fun before you get down on the floor to play with her. Your baby girl loves a good time and is now ready to show off her developing sense of humor (as you'll learn when she dumps her dish of food on the floor and laughs with glee).

At this age, babies love the anticipation of a surprise. Try the gonna-get-you game by wiggling your finger in the air as you musically say, "IIIII'm gonna get you!" And then gently poke your daughter's tummy and watch her squeal with delight.

Peek-a-boo is another favorite game of anticipation. If you get tired of hiding your face behind your hands, cover a toy and let her uncover it.

Singing games are always fun for your daughter because they're repetitive and predictable. "The itsy-bitsy spider" is an old-time favorite with fun hand movements that your daughter will soon try to imitate.

Body games are always fun. "This Little Piggy" and "Where are baby's eyes, nose, etc." are not only good for a hearty laugh, but they also help your daughter learn about her body.

Between four and seven months, your daughter's sense of humor will start to show. A game of peek-a-boo may have attracted her quiet interest in the past, but now will spark giggles with arms and legs waving in joy. And if you have an older child, your daughter will especially enjoy playing with him or her. One funny face from a sibling can give an infant a great belly laugh. But don't let them play unsupervised. An older sibling can very easily (and unintentionally) harm a baby. It would not be unusual for a three-year-old to wonder if a spoon inserted into one of the baby's ears would come out the other side!

Social Development

Infants between four and seven months are very social. You've seen your daughter bubble with happiness when even a stranger stops to say hello. Each social interaction teaches her that she is someone special and that she can have an effect on the world around her. Having the opportunity to be among people helps your child learn who she is and how she fits into her world.

You might even consider setting up a playdate for your little one. When my daughter was still an infant, I had a good friend with a daughter the same age. We often got together for a cup of tea and some adult company. We'd put our daughters down on a blanket and turn our attention to our own conversation. It sure didn't look like much was happening between the girls at these little playdates. They lay or sat next to each other and entertained themselves with their own rattles or toes. I didn't realize at the time (but have learned since!) that these social get-togethers were just as good for my daughter as they were for me.

Developmental experts tell us that side-by-side play with other babies gives infants opportunities to get used to being with other children, to watch them, and to imitate their actions. These are important first steps toward learning how to interact with others. Given the opportunity to play with the same child regularly, even infants can become friends.

Get Ready to Run

Rest time is over. As your daughter moves into the eight- to eleven-month age group discussed in the next chapter, she's ready to hit the road. She'll be creeping, crawling, walking, and running before you know it—with you following right behind. So get out your track shoes and get ready for some fast-paced adventures!

MY BABY GIRL

"Although I love my two boys, I'm so glad I also have a daughter. Having another female in the house makes me feel very happy and optimistic about the future."

—Lori Sulioz
mother of a little girl

"I have three girls, and my mother also had three girls, so I can give you one million reasons why girls are so great! Here are a few:

- Watching how much fun they have playing dress-up as their favorite princess.

- Finding little pink socks all over the house.

- Having a huge collection of princess movies.

- Trying to be creative with their hair and knowing it will always turn out cute!

- Watching them make new friends with other little girls.

- Playing with their dolls."

—Kristen Garza
mother of three little girls

Four

On the Move:

Your Daughter from Eight to Eleven Months

My Colleen was a girl who liked to be in constant motion. As an infant, she loved her automatic swing. She then moved on to the joys of a Jolly Jumper, which was a seat suspended on elasticized ropes from the doorframe that let her jump up and down to her heart's delight. She then graduated to a walker on wheels, which I know are no longer recommended, for safety reasons, but Colleen loved hers because it let her keep up with her brothers. Thankfully she met with no disasters. Of course, once she figured out how to crawl, there was no stopping her exciting exploration of the world.

Unlike her whirlwind brothers, however, Colleen was the quiet and inquisitive type. She would roam around until she found something that interested her (such as a forgotten shoe or bracelet) and then stop to examine, ponder, and experience it with all her senses. I didn't realize at the time that this was an early glimpse at her emerging personality. Over the years, she continued to be the still waters that run deep.

Your daughter may be calm and introspective like mine, or she may be trouble on wheels. Either way, during these months you're both learning a lot about each other, so make sure you take time every once in a while to sit back and admire the unique and grand person she is becoming.

Feeding Basics

Your daughter's eating habits will dramatically change during these few months. Her staple diet will move from liquid to solid foods and she may switch from bottle or breast to a cup. These changes give her lots of experiences with the taste, texture, and enjoyment of food that make for lively mealtimes!

WEANING FROM BOTTLE OR BREAST

There's no rule about when a baby should stop breast- or bottle-feeding. My boys switched to solid foods and a sippy cup around their first birthday, but my daughter clung to her bottle until past two. (In fact, when she began carrying around her juice bottle as if it were a favorite blanket, my husband and I decided to "lose" it on a family outing.)

As you begin to introduce solid foods, your daughter will let you know what she needs. You might find that she does not want to nurse or bottle-feed as often. If this happens, you should cut back one feeding at a time, starting perhaps with a midday meal (because this tends to be the smallest and least convenient feeding).

Most parents hold on to the last feeding before bed for quite a while after the first birthday. Others continue to provide bottle or breast milk "snacks" at the baby's request until she loses interest.

If you are breast-feeding, you may decide at this time to completely wean your daughter. This should be done slowly so that your breasts have a chance to adjust. If you suddenly stop, they will become engorged with milk and that can be very painful. Cut out one breast-milk feeding a day at first and then two, and so on. If your daughter is not yet a year old, you should switch to formula rather than cow's milk even if you wean your daughter off the breast to a cup.

Here are some guidelines to help you decide if it's time to wean from bottle or breast:

☐ Has your daughter lost the tongue-thrust reflex that caused her to instinctively push things out of her mouth? Does she easily, without gagging, swallow pureed foods? If so, she may be ready for the switch.

☐ Is your daughter able to sit up by herself? This is a good indicator that she's ready to sit down for a good meal.

☐ Does your daughter reach out to grab for food? This could be a sign that she'd like to experiment with nonliquid foods.

A TOTALLY SOLID FOOD DIET

Once you have introduced a variety of single foods (as discussed in the last chapter), you can start to mix it up, serving a combination of fruits, cereals, and vegetables (still thoroughly pureed, of course).

When your daughter can sit on her own and is handling pureed food well, you can start offering coarser textures. You can also start introducing finger foods. Be sure these are soft and cut into small pieces—she will either swallow them whole or let them dissolve in her mouth. Favorite finger foods include bits of cooked carrots, potatoes, or peas, bits of whole-wheat bread or crackers, and Cheerios or a similar cereal. (At first you'll find that your daughter smushes, spatters, and throws far more food than she eats. It's all part of the learning process.)

Many children are prone to gagging and even throwing up when they are learning to eat. This may happen if your daughter has too much food in her mouth or if she encounters a new taste or surprising texture, like a lump hidden in smooth pudding. If this happens to your daughter, give her only small amounts and continued experiences with foods of different textures. If the gagging reflex continues, be sure to mention it to her doctor.

DRINKING FROM A CUP

This is the time that many babies like to experiment with drinking from a cup with a spouted lid. When you first offer a cup to your daughter, don't expect a civilized reaction. She will shake it, bang it, and throw it—so it's best to fill it with just a bit of water at first.

Demonstrate how to use it and encourage her to sip from the spout. Once she gets the hang of it, you can then offer breast milk, formula, or water to drink from the cup.

Once your daughter is eating fruit, you can try fruit juice, but don't overdo it—it's better for babies to learn to eat fruit (which has more fiber) and drink water (which has no sugar) than to get them bonded to juice (which has a lot of sugar and sometimes causes diarrhea). The sweet taste of fruit juice can seduce some children into becoming habitual high-volume juice drinkers, crowding more nutrition-rich foods out of their diets. A baby of one year, for instance, shouldn't drink more than about four ounces of juice a day. In fact, it's fine for a baby to drink no juice at all, as long as she eats fruit.

For ease of use, try giving your daughter a two-handled cup, either open on top or with a top that has a spout. Some baby cups have a valve in the spout that prevents spills, allowing the liquid to come out only when the baby sucks it. These are neater, but be sure you clean the spout thoroughly. And switch off with other cups so the baby also gets to sip, rather than only suck.

Disciplining with Love

As your daughter grows, she'll become more mobile and assertive, but she can't mentally understand consequences or consciously control behavior. She will invariably want to do dangerous or disruptive things, such as pulling on curtains and electrical cords, but she's far too young to be punished for this. She has no way of understanding why you would slap her hand when she grabs hold of

SCIENCE SAYS

Even as an infant, researchers say your daughter is learning to separate people into male and female. To test whether an infant can tell men and women apart, the infant is typically shown slides or photos of female faces until she becomes bored and merely glances at each new example as if to say, "Another one of those? I've seen that already." Then she is shown a male face to see whether she shows renewed interest, which indicates that she recognizes that something different is being presented. Studies using this method have shown that by six months of age, infants can distinguish between male and female faces.

the curtain. She doesn't connect a loud scolding with putting something dangerous in her mouth. And certainly, she's too young to obey your "Don't touch" warning.

Your best approach in helping your daughter behave at this age is to distract her from potentially harmful situations with fun activities, music, or a favorite toy. When you see her cruising toward the electrical outlet, firmly say "No," turn her body around, and grab her attention with a new game or toy. If your daughter is pestering the family dog, say, "No," and then take her or the dog out of the room. Although your daughter is too young to completely understand what she did wrong, she will soon learn the word *no*. In fact, "no" is often one of a baby's very first words soon followed by a shake of the head. At first she won't know what the word means, but because she hears it so often, it's easy to repeat. And it is much easier for babies to shake their head from side to side than it is for them to nod up and down, so she will respond to almost anything you say with what seems like a negative. She's just practicing for the terrible twos when she finally knows what "no" means and likes to use it a lot.

Although your daughter is too young to understand the consequences of putting her finger into an electrical outlet, she is starting to learn how the things she does affect you. Just to see how you will react, she might experiment with behaviors such as pulling your hair, biting, poking, and high-pitched screaming. If you overreact, you can inadvertently encourage your daughter to repeat the behavior—strong reactions are exciting to babies and experienced as positive reinforcement rather than punishment.

Instead, if your daughter is screaming just to get attention, ignore her until she stops. When she does, reward her with hugs and kisses; rewarding good behavior can be a powerful tool for discipline. If your daughter is biting or poking, stay calm, firmly let her know, "No, that hurts," and restrain her for a few moments. If she persists, then put her down for a few moments and explain your actions in simple words.

You can best lay the foundation for later discipline by showering your daughter with love and attention. Have no fear—you can't spoil a child this young. Use this special time of infancy to make your child feel loved and important, which will in turn teach her about feelings of love for you. By the time your daughter is a toddler and ready for firmer discipline, she will be more likely to listen because she wants to please you.

Goodnight, My Baby

My daughter was a good sleeper from the day she was born. But my son Joe was a whole other story. Maybe your daughter is more like Joe: he never wanted to go to bed—ever. We'd put him in his crib, tiptoe out, and then brace for the scream that would follow.

Through my research, interviews, and writings on parenting issues, I've since learned that because babies have no idea when they're supposed to go to sleep, they need us to set the stage and make bedtime predictable and routine. By eight months, your daughter's biological clock has kicked into gear, so she's certainly ready to respond to a consistent bedtime ritual that is both pre-

SLEEP-DEPRIVED AND CRANKY

On its website www.sleepforkids.org, the National Sleep Foundation says that our babies no longer sleep like a baby. They have found that babies average almost ninety minutes less sleep a day than the fourteen-hour minimum that doctors recommend. It's not that they're going to sleep later or getting up earlier, but rather the quality of their sleep is disturbed throughout the night due to trouble falling asleep, heavy snoring, waking up at night, nightmares, and restless leg syndrome (involving unpleasant sensations in the legs, like itching and tingling). Sleep experts say infants and toddlers need enough sleep to remain alert and open to the world around them, and they attribute the problem to the current hectic patterns of daily life.

dictable and soothing and that will help her fall asleep at the same time every night.

A bedtime ritual consists of anything you'd like to do as you routinely put your daughter to bed for the night. A typical ritual might go something like this: You carry your daughter to the bedroom, turn on a night-light, sit to sing a lullaby, kiss a few stuffed animals goodnight, kiss your daughter, and lay her in her bed. Say goodnight and leave the room while she is still awake. After doing this repeatedly, your daughter will know it's time for bed as soon as you turn on the night-light. Same time, same place, same routine every night. The sameness of the ritual carries comfort, security, and a promise that the separation caused by sleep is predictable and temporary.

Whatever rituals you create, make sure they're ones you can repeat and pass on to your child's caregivers. If you build a routine that includes a story, a song, and a night-light, your spouse and babysitter will never get your child to sleep if they don't follow the same steps (in the same order). These are signals that tell your daughter what to do next; without these signals, children lose their sense of security and control.

Maybe the reason my daughter was such a good sleeper was because when she came along, I was determined not to repeat the bedtime mistakes I had made with her brother. This bedtime ritual worked like a charm with her. Live and learn.

Medical Care

Poison, toothcare, antibiotics, ear infections, and urinary tract infections: you may face all of these with your child during this period. These months will keep you hopping as you try to give your little girl room to grow and at the same time keep her safe and healthy.

ROUTINE AT-HOME CARE

Prevention is the key to good health in this time of late infancy. Planning ahead will help you combat the following two common problems before they even begin.

Poison Control: Now that your little girl is finding her way around, you should literally batten down the hatches. The combination of her mobility and her instinct to put everything in her mouth for exploration can be deadly if she consumes a toxic household substance or medication.

To make sure your daughter isn't one of the 1.2 million children younger than six years who ingest potentially poisonous substances each year, the website www.KidsHealth.org recommends these helpful tips:

☐ Store all medications, vitamins, cleaning supplies, and alcoholic drinks in high (preferably locked) cabinets. Cosmetics and toiletries should also be kept far from your daughter's reach.

☐ Never tell a child that medicine is "candy."

☐ Take special precautions when you have houseguests. Be sure their medications are far from reach, preferably locked in one of their bags.

OUT WITH IPECAC

If you have a bottle of ipecac syrup in your medicine closet, throw it out. That's the most recent recommendation from the American Academy of Pediatrics. This syrup has long been recommended to induce vomiting in children who have swallowed poison or accidentally overdosed on medication. But the Academy has cancelled this recommendation because there are some poisoning situations where vomiting can actually be more harmful to the child, and because any baby who has ingested poison or medication should be rushed to the hospital whether vomiting is induced or not. Instead, it is recommended that parents focus on poison prevention in their homes and keep this number for Poison Control handy: 800-222-1222.

☐ Don't rely on packaging to protect your daughter. *Child-resistant* does not mean *childproof*.

☐ Keep medications and cleaning supplies in their original containers—not in old soda bottles or containers that were once used for food.

☐ While cleaning or using household chemicals, never leave the bottles unattended if a small child is present. Similarly, take special care with alcohol during parties—guests may not be conscious of where they've left their drinks.

☐ Keep rat poison or roach powders off the floors of your home.

☐ Keep hazardous automotive and gardening products in a securely locked area in your garage.

☐ Learn all the names of the plants in your house and remove any that could be toxic.

☐ Discard used button-cell batteries safely and store any used ones far from children's reach (alkaline substances are poisonous).

(This information was provided by KidsHealth, one of the largest resources online for medically reviewed health information written for parents, kids, and teens. For more articles like this one, visit www.KidsHealth.org or www.TeensHealth.org. © 1995–2004. The Nemours Foundation.)

Tooth Care: By the time your girl is eleven months old, she is likely to have her two bottom and two top teeth as well as her upper and lower side teeth. That's why it's time for your baby girl's first visit to the dentist! The American Dental Association and the American Academy of Pediatric Dentists recommend that children see a dentist by age one, when they generally have about six to eight teeth. Dentists say that dental problems in young children may be difficult for parents to spot, so even though the teeth look fine to you, there may be early signs of trouble that a dentist can detect. Also, a dentist experienced in treating young children can give you extra guidance on how to clean those little teeth and how to prevent future problems.

If you decide to take your daughter to a dentist at this young age, it's best to find a pediatric dentist with special training in dealing with children, or a family dentist who has a lot of experience with kids. An office that caters to children generally will have interesting toys and books in the waiting room, hygienists who know how to talk to young children, and cheerful props and take-home goodies.

This first visit will be for a checkup only. Your daughter will sit on your lap and if she hasn't developed a severe case of stranger anxiety just yet, she will probably enjoy looking around at the new environment while the dentist examines her teeth. This should be a pleasant visit without discomfort or fear that can help your child avoid an early case of dentist-phobia.

ROUTINE CHECKUPS

Your daughter may look perfectly healthy to you, but she still needs to see her doctor for routine checkups. As your daughter finishes up her first year, the American Academy of Pediatrics recommends a well-baby exam at nine months of age.

Just like the previous health checkups, your daughter's doctor will give your daughter a complete once-over. She will:

☐ Record your daughter's physical growth: her weight, length, and head circumference will be measured.

☐ Flash a light in your daughter's eyes to monitor pupil dilation. She will also move the light from side to side, asking your child to follow the light with her eyes. She is looking to see if they wander, cross, or move in different directions—all signs of strabismus, a common, often correctable childhood eye problem.

☐ Examine the ears, checking behind the eardrum for fluid and the middle ear for redness, swelling, or other signs of infection.

☐ Look inside the nose, checking nasal membranes for swelling due to a cold or allergy and the mucus for color and consistency (this may indicate infection).

☐ Open the mouth wide to check the throat, and tonsils for bumps, sores, swelling, or color changes—all signs of infection.

☐ Use a stethoscope to listen to your daughter's heart for rate and rhythm, and lungs for any respiratory problems.

☐ Feel your daughter's abdomen to rule out abnormal masses or enlarged organs and check for gurgling sounds of the intestinal tract.

☐ Check the genitalia for any signs of tenderness or infection.

This visit also gives you a good opportunity to discuss any health concerns you may have. If you're wondering if your daughter's physical development, large motor skills, language skills, feeding schedule, or sleeping patterns are on track, ask. Your daughter's doctor sees many infants every day and cannot know what child development issues are most important to each parent. If at all possible, both parents should accompany the baby. This lets both of you get to know the person charged with caring for your daughter's health and also offers an extra hand so that at least one of you can listen to the doctor's advice without being distracted.

COMMON HEALTH CONCERNS

As you watch your daughter grow, you will routinely deal with normal health concerns such as sniffles, colds, bumps, and bruises. But when your daughter has an ear or urinary tract infection you should visit her doctor for proper treatment, which may or may not include a course of antibiotics.

Ear Infections: Popular literature says that ear infections (medical term: otitis media) account for 24.5 million doctor visits each year and are the second most common childhood ailment, following upper respiratory infections. So what causes these common infections?

When a baby lies flat, the Eustachian tube—the tube that connects the back of the throat with the middle ear—is more horizontal. This allows fluid and germs to travel more easily from the back of the throat to the middle ear. This tube is shorter in babies and so the fluid more easily finds its way into that middle ear. That's why if your daughter has a head cold it may lead to an ear infection if fluids back up into the ear, giving the germs that cause ear infections a nice, warm place to grow. Even fluid like formula or breast milk or juice that a baby drinks while lying down can do the same thing.

Oddly enough, allergens can also cause ear infections. The allergens in cigarette smoke, for example, trigger secretions to plug the breathing passages and the Eustachian tube, setting up fluid in the middle ear ripe for possible infection. In fact, even allergens from pet dander can trigger secretions that build up in the middle ear and lead to infection.

So, if your daughter is prone to ear infections:

1. Always feed her upright (at no less than 30 degrees) and keep her upright for at least thirty minutes after a feeding.

2. Keep her away from cigarette smoke.

3. Keep pets out of her bedroom (and, certainly, don't let the baby and your pet sleep together in the same room).

Because ear infections are so common in young children, there's a good chance that your little girl will experience this discomfort. You should suspect an ear infection if your daughter shows these symptoms:

☐ Irritability. Your daughter may cry and pull on one ear or the side of her face.

☐ Unwillingness to lie down (this increases the pain).

☐ Fever ranging from 100 to 104 degrees.

☐ Balance problems.

If you suspect an ear infection, get your daughter to the doctor for an accurate diagnosis. In some cases the infection is minor and will heal itself. In other cases there can be dangerous consequences if an ear infection is left untreated. Let the doctor decide. If there is no imminent danger, it's possible that because of the rampant overuse of antibiotics, the prescribed treatment will be quite different than it was for babies just one generation ago.

If my babies had slight fevers, acted irritable, and pulled on their ears, I could call the doctor's office and get a prescription for an antibiotic over the phone. Today, most physicians are hesitant to prescribe so quickly and prefer a "wait-and-see" approach. In fact, the American Academy of Pediatrics and the American Academy of Family Physicians has issued guidelines with a specific definition of what constitutes an ear infection and how to best treat it. Because it has been found that most children with an acute ear infection will get better without antibiotic treatment, the guidelines call for watchful waiting. They suggest that physicians give children a prescription for antibiotics only if they do not feel better in two days. Doctors aren't withholding antibiotics in cases where there is clearly an infection and the child is feverish and in pain, or in instances where the baby has a history of ear infections, but if the diagnosis is borderline, your daughter's physician may ask you to hold off on the antibiotics.

Whether you treat an ear infection with antibiotics or not, here are a few tips to help your daughter feel more comfortable:

☐ Don't put over-the-counter eardrops or warm water in your daughter's ear.

☐ Keep your daughter in a sitting position as much as possible. Sitting upright relieves pressure against the eardrum.

☐ Offer fluids to drink. Swallowing can open the inner ear tube and relieve pressure.

☐ With your daughter's doctor's approval, offer children's strength acetaminophen to relieve pain.

Urinary Tract Infection: Little girls are far more likely to get a urinary tract infection (UTI) than boys. The culprit in these infections (specifically cystitis) is *E. coli* and other bacteria that enter the urinary tract through the urethra (the tube that leads up to the bladder). In a female this bacteria can easily travel from the rectum to the urethra from the bowel movement in her diaper or when you clean her after a bowel movement, wiping from back to front. Boys rarely get cystitis, primarily because their urethra is located so far away from their rectum.

Sometimes the only symptom of a UTI is a fever that seems to appear for no reason and won't go away. Other symptoms can include irritability, loss of appetite, and vomiting. If your little girl has any of these symptoms be sure to call her doctor. If UTI is diagnosed it will be treated with prescribed antibiotics.

UTI RESOURCE

If your daughter has persistent urinary tract infections, you can get more information about UTIs from the American Foundation for Urologic Disease, at www.afud.org or 800-242-2383.

Overuse of Antibiotics: The most pressing reason why your daughter's doctor may hesitate to prescribe an antibiotic is that overuse and inappropriate use has caused this class of medication to lose some of its effectiveness. Newer antibiotic-resistant strains of bacterial infections have emerged. As a result, some commonly prescribed antibiotics are no longer reliable defenders against such common ailments as ear and sinus infections, tonsillitis, pneumonia, and tuberculosis.

Your daughter is at risk for developing resistance to antibiotics if:

1. She is given many courses of antibiotic treatments to treat frequent illnesses.

2. You stop a prescribed antibiotic treatment before completing the full dose. (This allows infectious bacteria that have not been killed to produce antibiotic-resistant offspring, and she may suffer a relapse that does not respond to the medication.)

To make sure your daughter takes antibiotics safely, follow these steps:

☐ Do not expect your daughter's doctor to prescribe an antibiotic for the common cold or other viral infections. Antibiotics do not kill viruses.

☐ If your daughter's doctor prescribes an antibiotic, follow the instructions exactly. If the medication is to be given twice a

CHECK THE DOSAGE

The U.S. Pharmacopeia, a not-for-profit organization that promotes standards for medicines, says that each year thousands of children are given the wrong doses of medications. This often happens, they say, because of a simple miscalculation involving the child's weight. The proper doses of most medications are based on a child's age and weight in kilograms, but most of us know our child's weight in pounds. If you divide pounds by 2.2, you will convert the figure into kilograms and this will help you confirm with your daughter's doctor that the weight and dosage match.

day for ten days, make sure you comply, even if she appears to feel much better.

☐ If you miss a dose or two, call the doctor or pharmacist to find out if you should double up, continue anew, or stop completely.

☐ Don't keep leftover antibiotics. If used properly, there should be no leftovers. If there are, you cannot use "just a little" on another occasion without risking the possibility of creating a resistant strain of bacteria. Also, antibiotics lose their potency over time.

Physical Growth

If you can hold your little explorer still long enough to take a quiet moment and reflect back on her first year of life, you'll be amazed at what she has achieved in such a short period of time. Most little girls will have tripled their birth weight and doubled their height by the time they are one year old. They have developed their neuromuscular abilities from the head down, first learning to control the head and neck, then the torso. They can now roll over from a lying-down position and push themselves to sitting in an easy, smooth maneuver. Finally they gain control of the lower body as they crawl and prepare to walk. The physical growth and development in this period between eight and eleven months is just fascinating to watch!

RIGHTY OR LEFTY?

As your daughter learns to grab a crayon and make a few scribbles, you might see that she tends to use the same hand each time. She won't be absolutely sure about which hand she prefers until she's about six years old, though even at this early age some parents try to influence the outcome. But you really can't. Being a righty or a lefty isn't a choice that your daughter will make. Child development experts say that our nervous systems are preprogrammed for right- or left-handedness. In fact, they say that pushing your child to use a particular hand—by placing toys in her right hand or correcting her if she opts for her left—can lead to problems later with hand-eye coordination and dexterity. Let your daughter use whichever hand—or hands—she's most comfortable with.

If she is a lefty (which is more likely if there are other lefties in the family) she's in good company. Take a look at this impressive list of female southpaws: Caroline Kennedy, Natalie Cole, Melissa Manchester, Judy Garland, Whoopie Goldberg, Angelina Jolie, Cloris Leachman, Diane Keaton, Marilyn Monroe, Sarah Jessica Parker, Julia Roberts, Monica Seles, Helen Keller, and U.S. Supreme Court Justice Ruth Bader Ginsberg.

CREEPING, CRAWLING, AND WALKING

Babies sure find interesting ways to get around. In the last chapter we talked about early creeping when some infants wiggle or slither forward on their stomachs using only their arms or elbows and pulling their legs along. Others learn they can more quickly cover a greater distance by rolling. Some scooch forward while sitting and doing what's sometimes called "bottom shuffling." And there's a whole group who move only backwards!

Sometime between eight and eleven months, most babies will get up on all fours and crawl forward. Learning to crawl is a real trial-and-error process. At first your daughter may get herself into the crawling position and then make a hesitant attempt at movement by rocking or swaying forward. When she tries to move, her balance is unstable and she may fall over. Because her control over her arms and shoulders develop faster than her control over her legs, she may find herself crawling backward away from the object she's trying to reach. How frustrating! This can go on for several weeks until her leg coordination develops further.

When your daughter does get the hang of crawling—watch out! She's like a tornado with knees. Nothing on floor level is safe from her grasp. So once again do a child-proofing run-through by getting down on the floor and taking stock from your daughter's viewpoint. The greatest danger to crawlers is from uncovered electrical outlets, ungated stairways, and household cleaners, medications, and other toxic substances. You should also secure or eliminate lightweight furniture, hide or secure electrical cords that

BABY NEEDS A NEW PAIR OF SHOES

Now that your daughter is getting ready to walk by cruising around while holding on to furniture, be sure her footwear helps rather than hinders her progress:

☐ Wearing slippery socks on smooth surfaces makes it hard for babies to get around.

☐ Being barefoot gives your daughter the best traction (as long as she is in a clean, protected area).

☐ Buy her flexible shoes with smooth soles that won't grip the floor and cause your daughter to trip.

☐ Don't choose high-top shoes. They were thought to be the best choice years ago, but they limit ankle movement.

☐ Buy shoes that fit. If you allow too much "room to grow" the awkward feel will make it harder for your daughter to walk.

☐ Resist the stylish shoes (like baby cowgirl boots) that are not flexible or porous.

can be pulled on, and keep valuable and small objects that can be swallowed on high shelves or locked in cabinets. Then stand back. Your daughter's curiosity now has motor power!

Although it's important to remove dangerous items, you don't have to clear a path for your daughter to practice crawling. In fact, you can enhance her explorations by scattering pillows around the room for her to climb over or around. Put toys in corners for her to discover, and roll balls across the floor for her to chase. This is great fun for her and also good practice of motor coordination.

Most babies will crawl for a while and then practice walking by pulling themselves up on furniture, moving along while holding on for balance. They'll cruise around the room going from the sofa to the coffee table to the chair. Sometimes they'll let go and stand unsupported until gravity and a shaky sense of balance pulls them down. Soon, they will walk while holding on to you with both hands, and then with only one. Most take their first uncertain steps alone between the ages of nine and thirteen months. That's when the fun really begins!

Emotional Development

Between eight and eleven months, your daughter will deal with many different emotions. She is now realizing that her world is far bigger than herself and her immediate family—which can be a scary thing. And she's beginning to develop strong bonds to those she loves and becoming fearful of those she doesn't know. Eventually, with your love and patience, she'll grow to feel secure in this great big world.

SEPARATION ANXIETY

Until your daughter is about nine months old, she has no idea that you still exist when you walk out of the room. No wonder she screams when you try to leave her!

This fear of losing you is called separation anxiety and it causes most children around the age of ten months to become very clingy and fearful of separation. Around this time I nicknamed my baby girl Gumby. She felt like a piece of gum under my shoe because I couldn't take a step without her attached to me. If I dared to leave her sight, she would cry so pitifully with distress and anguish that it felt like she was reaching into my chest and pulling out my heart.

I felt slightly better when the pediatrician assured me that her dramatic reaction was quite normal and that she would outgrow this stage of intense separation anxiety. She also offered me some tips about how to help my daughter deal with these feelings. She said it was best not to give in to her fear by spending every moment at home together. "She needs to learn how to be apart from you," the doctor said. "She needs to know that you leave her—and you return."

You can help your daughter learn this lesson by continuing to play the separation games mentioned in Chapter 2. When your daughter is awake, say bye-bye, leave the room for a brief period of time, and then return with a smile and offer a cuddle. Do this often throughout the day, extending the amount of time you're out of sight each time. If your daughter immediately cries when you leave the room, try maintaining voice contact while you're out of sight.

When you do leave your child, don't let the separation and reunion become a dramatic scene. Say goodbye with a smile and leave quickly. (No running back to dry those tears and offer yet more reassurances.) When you return, enter the room calmly with a happy face and offer a warm greeting without getting carried away with hugs and tears and a litany of how much you missed your child. Tearful, drawn-out separations and returns tell her that separation is a big deal and something to be worried about.

Your daughter's world is expanding and she is now able to separate experiences into those that make her feel comfortable and those that frighten her. This is a positive sign of development, but she needs your help to make these emotional adjustments. So try to be patient when she grabs on and won't let go.

STRANGER ANXIETY

Along with separation anxiety comes stranger anxiety—yet another pull on your patience. I was flabbergasted when my daughter first pulled away and hid her face from anyone outside the immediate family who dared move in with a friendly coochi-coo. What had happened to my friendly little girl?

I later learned this reaction is what's known as stranger anxiety. On the up side of this developmental stage, the baby is learning to distinguish herself from others. She is starting to understand that certain people are familiar and safe—her parents, siblings, and babysitter are greeted with joyful smiles of recognition. But on the down side, a previously friendly baby who would delight strangers and distant relatives with her winning personality may now decide that unfamiliar faces are scary, and scream at the sight of a bearded man or absolutely refuse to be held by Aunt Bea, who wears glasses.

If your daughter develops stranger anxiety, don't worry that she's becoming antisocial or pathologically shy. It's a phase that will pass as she learns to feel more secure in her world. To get that sense of security, she may want to sit on your lap (and only your lap) when "strangers" are around, or she may hide her face in your shoulder when introduced to new people. If that happens, don't make a fuss. You won't encourage a sense of security by insisting that she let Aunt Bea hold her. In fact, making babies confront their fears at this age makes them more clingy and insecure.

Instead of pushing your daughter into social situations that frighten her, enjoy her clingy little grip around your neck and gently help her to let go. You can start by getting her out of the house so she gets to see lots of different people. When you introduce her to someone she doesn't know or feel comfortable with, keep her in your arms and let her get friendly with the person at her own pace (and accept that it may be a very slow pace). Give her lots of praise for her efforts even when she covers her face with her hands to hide.

You can also help by being friendly yourself. When you interact with other people, your little girl is watching you very closely. If you smile and appear relaxed when you talk to the checkout clerk at the grocery store or a visiting relative, your daughter will learn that these people are okay and that she can feel comfortable with them, too. She builds her sense of trust and security with others by observing you. So smile and relax if your little girl suddenly seems exceptionally shy. It's a sign that she's growing up and learning to be cautious.

Cognitive Development

Your daughter's intellectual growth marches forward during these months at incredible speed. Now she is the great imitator. She learns to feed herself by watching how others do it. She lets you wash her face with a washcloth and then will want to take the cloth to wash your face in return. She is learning how to use gestures to communicate and her memory is improving daily (she may now even remember where she left her favorite toy). Every waking moment is a learning adventure.

ADVANTAGE GIRLS: STRONG LANGUAGE SKILLS

Your daughter is learning the language much faster than she's letting on. She may only say a few repeated syllables such as *dada* and *mama*, but her ability to understand language is far more advanced. This is called receptive language and it develops long before your daughter can put her own thoughts into words. With receptive language the two of you can communicate at a fairly advanced level. She'll now do a lot of pointing and gesturing in response to your words. When you say, "Where's Fido?" she'll point to the dog. When she wants to draw your attention to a toy, she'll pick it up and shake it in front of you. This is all part of language development.

If you compare your daughter's ability to talk with the vocabulary of a little boy of the same age, it's likely that your daughter will be far more advanced. While boys tend to take in the language

and mull it over for longer periods before they attempt it themselves, girls tend to jump right in and talk sooner and more.

Claire Lerner, LCSW, a child development specialist with the
national nonprofit organization Zero to Three (www.zero-
tothree.org), in Washington DC, which focuses on early childhood development, points out that this may be related to the
findings of research studies that say females tend to be more
relationship-oriented than males. "This is socialized into girls at a
very young age," says Lerner. "Part of connecting and socializing
is through talking. It's not clear if girls are born with a genetic
makeup that causes them to be more verbal or if their life experiences encourage this development. But the studies do show that
they definitely have the early verbal advantage."

Researcher and author Michael Gurian agrees. He has observed
that girls use more words during the learning process, while boys
more often work silently. "Even when we study student group processes, we find females in a learning group using words more than
males." And females, says Gurian, use more concrete, everyday
language than males. In his book *Boys and Girls Learn Differently*
Gurian notes: "Boys often find jargon and coded language more
interesting. As one brain researcher told me years ago, 'It's just not
as much of interest to females to create the kind of verbal obfusca-
tion legalese uses. If Western culture's founding lawyers and
judges had been women, judicial language would be easier to understand.'" I certainly agree!

As your daughter polishes up her language skills in these early
months, the best indicator of her language development is not the
number of words she can say, but rather how well she communi-

cates her thoughts, feelings, and needs in other ways. Facial expressions, gestures, and inflection in sounds all communicate. A child who is able to communicate effectively through actions and behaviors at this age is very likely to eventually attain strong language skills. To start she might also reach up to you to say "pick me up." Being able to organize this action to tell you what she wants is a very sophisticated form of communication that Lerner feels too many parents don't recognize for the advanced skill that it is. "Long before a child has words," she says, "watch for her early methods of communication. They are quite amazing."

PLAYTIME AND LEARNING

A child's play is her classroom. You can help your daughter develop her intellect by giving her age-appropriate toys that help her use her new ability to sort, organize, and problem-solve. These toys do not have to be high-tech electronic computerized devices. Simple sorting and stacking games are plenty challenging for this age group.

Between eight and nine months, your daughter may become fascinated with an activity board. These games let your daughter make things happen. If she pushes this button, she'll hear a certain noise. If she moves this lever, that object will pop up. If she puts her finger in that hole, this light will glow. It's like a science lab for your little one.

Between ten and eleven months, she'll be ready for more advanced experiments. A shape sorter, for example, will both fascinate and frustrate her. She will know that the blocks of various shapes go into the box, but at first she will use brute force to try forcing them into the wrong hole. With your help, slowly she will grasp the concept that she will be more successful if she matches the shape of the block to the shape of the hole.

Babies learn by imitating. So slowly and repeatedly show your daughter how to work these kinds of toys and then give her room to try. Let her feel some frustration before you jump in to help so she learns the value of persistence—something in shorter supply in girls than in boys because parents are often less willing to let their little girls struggle.

NOW YOU SEE IT, NOW YOU DON'T

Object permanence is an advanced intellectual concept for little babies. Around nine months of age, they begin to understand that just because an object is hidden, doesn't mean it has disappeared. In the past, if you placed a toy under a blanket, your daughter would turn away, assuming the toy was gone. Now, she will pull at the blanket looking for the hidden toy.

This awareness becomes a favorite game. You'll see how delighted your little girl will be when she finds a hidden object. She

---

IT'S ALL IN THE BRAIN

The parietal lobe of the brain interprets sensations such as touch, pain, and temperature. The female brain in infants seems more attuned to sensory input than males, making baby girls more sensitive to physical sensations on the skin.

will enjoy placing an object in a box and then shaking the box to make it "reappear." Games of peek-a-boo and hide-and-seek are also playful ways to teach the reassuring reality of object permanence. Your daughter may not be ready for a neighborhood game of hide-and-seek, but she'll be delighted when you play "Where's the stuffed animal?"

ANOTHER REASON TO TURN OFF THE TV

The value of children's television has long been controversial, but here's some news about kids and TV watching that takes the debate in a whole new direction. Researchers at the Children's Hospital and Regional Medical Center in Seattle have found that it's not the content of the TV shows we should be most concerned about, but rather, the amount of TV viewing time. They found that very young children who watch television face an increased risk of attention deficit problems by school age. They say that the unrealistically fast-paced visual images typical of most TV programming may overstimulate and permanently "rewire" the developing brain.

These findings were based on astounding study results. Researchers found that for every hour of television watched daily, children aged one to three faced a 10 percent increased risk of having attention problems at age seven. That means that if my daughter watches three hours of TV a day, her risk of attention deficit problems jumps 30 percent over children who watch no TV.

This is not the first time the negative effects of TV on young children have been noted. Earlier studies have found that television can shorten attention spans, affect brain growth and the development of social, emotional, and cognitive skills, and also contribute to the epidemic of obesity and aggressiveness. In fact, in 1999 the American Academy of Pediatrics said that children under the age of two should not watch television at all. That kind of serious news should be plastered all over every TV sold: "Warning: TV watching can be dangerous to children's mental health."

Social Development

The way your daughter responds to family, friends, and strangers is, in part, determined by her temperament. Does she reach out to everyone she meets? Or does she draw back? Is she friendly or sociable? Or does she get upset by new people and places? Knowing your daughter's temperament will help you better understand why she acts the way she does in social situations.

ALL GIRLS ARE NOT THE SAME

How would you describe a baby girl? Ask a dozen adults this question and you'll find that many will use adjectives such as cute, cuddly, happy, and the like. But actually, these are characteristics of temperament based on stereotypes that have nothing to do with gender. Although girls do tend to be calmer and less aggressive than boys (as we'll see in Chapter 5), expecting your daughter to act "like a girl" is setting you both up for trouble.

Whether your child is "easy," "difficult," or "slow to warm up," the message she gets about whether or not she's accepted and loved comes partly from the way you respond to her unique temperament. Unfortunately, if a child doesn't fit an expected gender stereotype, the response from parents sometimes sends the message that "You are not loved unless you act the way I expect you to act."

Let's say, for example, that two different parents bring their ten-month-old girls to the park one day. One little girl is scrambling all around, will never sit still, and is very aggressive with the other children (meaning pushing kids out of the way). The second little girl is sitting quietly near her mother, holding her stuffed animal, and being polite and kind to the other children. If the parent of the first little girl expects girls to be calm and polite she will think there is something wrong. The parent will scold her daughter for running around and insist that she play nearby. When the child resists, the parent may show anger or annoyance. The little girl will have no idea what she did wrong, but she'll know that something about who she is has upset her parent.

Researchers have found that very often parents tend to be more accepting of boys who are very active and mischievous and less accepting of these traits in their girls. Boys who never sit still are admired; girls who do the same need to be tamed. These expectations can have a strong influence on the child's behavior and sense of self-esteem.

To better understand the way stereotypes can affect the way you raise your daughter, child development specialist Claire Lerner suggests these three important steps:

- **Recognize your expectations of a girl.** These are not good or bad, right or wrong. They are simply ideas you carry in your mind that cause you to act in certain ways that can be harmful to your relationship with your daughter if your expectations don't match hers. If you are a kind, calm, and nurturing person, for example, you may expect your daughter to be the same, especially because she's "a girl."

■ **Understand who your child is.** Avoid "girl" labels based on stereotypes and instead tune into your daughter's cues: What makes her tick? How does she react to certain situations? You are the one who can best know what her preferences are, what scares her, what makes her happy. Using this information, you can respond to her in ways that effectively meet her needs.

"For children's developing sense of self-esteem and self-confidence, it is critical that they get accepting messages from their parents," Lerner says. "They need to know, even at this young age, that they are okay. That they are not 'wrong' or 'bad' if they prefer to play rough and tumble games rather than quiet ones."

■ **Work with both your expectations and her personality.** Use what you know about yourself and what you know about your daughter to find ways that make you both happy without feeling either disappointed or shamed. First encourage your daughter to explore her world in a way that makes her comfortable. Then, if you'd like your active daughter to be a bit calmer, you can find ways that are not pushy or disrespectful to engage her in those kinds of quieter activities. If she likes to run around in a whirlwind of movement, you can encourage quiet play by building "time-out" periods into her play. Show her the fun of taking a rest and playing with a coloring book or clay for a short period before she runs off again. This isn't forcing her to be someone she's not; it's a way to broaden her experiences by showing her how she can enjoy quiet as well as active play. The key is to do this in small doses without forcing your daughter against her will to act in ways that meet *your* expectations.

Enjoy the unique person your little girl is growing into by putting aside any labels you attach to the word *girl* and encourage lots of experiences that allow her to develop at her own speed and in areas that she (not only her parents) enjoys.

"EASY," "DIFFICULT," AND "SLOW-TO-WARM-UP" BABIES

When my little girl was born, she cried inconsolably round the clock. At our first baby checkup, the doctor found that she had a raging ear infection that had punctured her eardrum. "Hasn't she been crying a lot?" the doctor grimly asked. Of course she had, but her older brother was a screamer by personality so I thought it was natural. After a round of antibiotics, my daughter quieted down and spent her days smiling and cooing with glee. I learned the hard way that babies have very distinct temperaments, and knowing that temperament helps parents better meet their children's needs.

There is scientific evidence that infants do possess distinct temperaments that dictate the way they react to their parents, to other people, and to their environment. In the 1950s, child development researchers Alexander Thomas and Stella Chess began a now famous thirty-year study out of New York University Medical Center. They followed 133 infants from birth to adulthood and found that children do come equipped with their own unique personalities. Today, most child-development experts agree, and find that the most successful and satisfied parents are those who can adjust their parenting strategies to complement their child's temperament.

In this study (and in today's infant population as well) approximately 40 percent of the children were "easy" babies who followed regular schedules, had a positive approach to change, and experienced only mild mood swings. Ten percent were "difficult" babies who followed irregular schedules, had intense reactions to change, and experienced frequent negative moods. And 15 percent were "slow-to-warm-up" babies who were cautious, had a mildly negative response to new situations, and needed to approach strangers and situations slowly. The remainder showed combinations of temperament traits that did not fit neatly into one of these three categories.

What kind of baby girl do you have? Take time during this infant period to observe your daughter and try to understand how she interacts with her world. The following descriptions are from a book I wrote with child psychologist Charles Schaefer called *Raising Baby Right*. They are very general and apply to a baby's most common behaviors.

Difficult Babies: Kick and cry during diaper changes; awake three or four times during the night; cry inconsolably during a trip to the supermarket; pull away and scream when a stranger approaches; awakes instantly if the phone rings; if hungry will scream frantically before you have a chance to offer food; will stop feeding to turn toward a noise; will spend most of the day crying.

Easy Babies: Lie quietly during diaper changes; will sleep between midnight and 5 A.M.; will enjoy a trip to the supermarket and will seem interested in the changing environment; will smile and reach toward a stranger; will sleep through the phone ringing; when hungry will make sucking noises or suck on her fingers without much complaining; will not be distracted from feeding by noise in the room; spends most of the day in a pleasant mood.

Slow-to-Warm-Up Babies: Wiggle and squirm during diaper changes; will awake once or twice between midnight and 5 A.M.; will cry when she first enters a store, but then calm down with only occasional whimpers of complaint; will fuss and shy away from a stranger; will whimper or cry out if the phone rings while she is sleeping, but will then fall back to sleep; when hungry will cry on and off until you offer food; will slow the sucking pace if she hears noise while feeding but will then continue.

The advantage of knowing your daughter's temperament is not so you can change her to fulfill your expectations. It is, instead, having an opportunity to create a good fit between your temperament and your child's. This becomes especially important when temperament gets mixed up with stereotypical labels that define how a little girl "should" act.

Full Speed Ahead

Your baby girl is now leaving infancy behind and moving full speed ahead into toddlerhood. But before she goes, she leaves you with a year full of exciting "firsts," magical moments, and memories of messy faces, silly laughs, and sloppy kisses.

MY BABY GIRL

"My eleven-month-old daughter is a gift from God. I love waking up to her beautiful face and the words *up Mama*. She makes all of my struggles fade away. She is the beat of my heart, which keeps me living."

—Kimberly Marone

"My daughter was clingy and extremely loving until when reached the age of thirteen. Then she became very critical of me. It was as if I was her competition. When she was out on her own at eighteen, she quickly came back around to be that sweet, loving girl I remembered."

—Shawn Elton

Five

Toddler Time:

Your Daughter from Twelve to Eighteen Months . . . and Beyond

It's impossible to look at the cherubic face of a sleeping baby girl and not smile. At this age, she is so deliciously cuddly and huggable—when she's sleeping. When she is awake, it's a whole other story! Your little girl is now gaining the muscle strength and coordination to run, jump, and climb all over her world, and she won't want to slow down and risk wasting a single minute of any day.

This is a wonderful stage of rapid growth, intellectual leaps, and emotional ups and downs that will whiz by in a flash. So take lots of pictures. It's the only way you'll remember all of the wonderful moments you're in for during these precious years.

Calm Little Girls

In the first year of life, your daughter is just as active as any baby boy. All babies kick their arms and legs, roll around, crawl, and cruise with equal vigor. But after the first birthday, girls tend to calm down while boys ratchet up the action. Of course each child is unique and certainly there are some perfectly healthy girls who never sit still and some boys who prefer quiet play to rough-housing, but there are plenty of studies showing that most often it's the boys who have a higher activity level.

Scientists, who are always curious to know why things like this happen, have conducted studies that point to hormones. Although there's no doubt that many boys are socialized to be more active by the games their parents and friends play with them, there are some noteworthy studies that say it's highly likely that many girls are less active due to their hormones.

These results first come out of animal studies. Juvenile male rodents as well as monkeys show a high level of rough-and-tumble play or play fighting. This consists of boisterous activity with lots of body contact. Juvenile females normally show very little of this behavior. Alice Sterling Honig, Ph.D., professor emerita of child and family studies in the College of Human Services and Health Professions at Syracuse University, believes that all male mammals who are primates have a higher activity level than females. "Go to the zoo," she says, "and you will see the male monkeys climbing around faster and more frequently than females. Their activity level is noticeably higher. The same is true for human males, too."

The cause, say many, may be the level of sex hormones a child is exposed to before birth and their effect on the brain. Males and females produce both androgens (the male hormone) and estrogen (the female hormone), but as we'll see later in this chapter the androgen levels are higher in males than in females. This increase may be the reason for the higher activity levels in males. Scientists who have studied personality in girls agree. They have found that females born with higher than average androgen levels are more "tomboyish" than other girls and are more active in sports involving rough body contact (and oddly enough, prefer trucks over dolls). There is some early evidence that extremely high androgen levels in females may affect gender orientation, but these studies are in the very early stages. It is generally agreed, however, that the slightly higher androgen levels seem to make about 20 percent of females more "masculine" in their actions and thinking processes than other girls, but do not predict homosexual tendencies.

This explains why even the act of coloring was a different experience for my daughter than for my sons. My daughter was perfectly happy to sit down and color a picture. My sons would sit, then jump up, then sit down, then kick their legs back and forth, then move to another chair, then change position to kneel on the chair, then drop the crayons and jump off the chair to pick them up, and the climb back onto the chair, and then break the crayons into pieces, and so on until it was time to move on to another activity. After these two wore me down, I was very happy that my youngest was a little girl who, although full of life and energy, could at least sit still until the end of a storybook.

Toilet Training

We all know that none of our kids will arrive at their high school graduation in diapers. But for some of us, the process of getting them toilet trained can seem so long and difficult that it's almost impossible to imagine that day.

My daughter was almost two and a half years old when she announced that she didn't want to wear diapers anymore. I had not even begun to toilet train her because we were in the process of moving to a new house and timing potty trips and cleaning accidents would have been too much for me at this time. But Colleen insisted she was ready. I bargained with her for just a little more time. "When we move into the new house," I promised, "we'll throw away the diapers and you'll use the toilet like a big girl." A few weeks later, we walked into our new home weighted down with stacks of boxes as, Colleen ran through the house yelling, "Where's the bathroom? Where's the bathroom?" She was ready.

The decision about when to start toilet training is a very individual one that depends on personal, social, and even day-care factors. But there is no one "right" time. In the 1920s and 1930s, many parents used a very strict and early approach that is far different from what most parents use today. A 1935 publication by the U.S. Children's Bureau suggested that toilet training should begin shortly after birth. "If not," it continued, "it should always be begun by the third month and be completed by the eighth month." Can you imagine even trying that? In the 1940s and 1950s, attitudes became a bit more permissive and parents were encouraged to wait until the child was eight months old to begin training. Then, when most households had their own washing machines in the 1960s and when diapers became disposable in the 1970s, toilet training moved into the second and third year, when a child is most capable of controlling these physical functions.

Here are some general guidelines about timing that I learned while writing the book called *Toilet Training Without Tears* with Charles Schaefer, Ph.D. They may help you better understand your child's capabilities at this time:

One Year: A child may attain dryness after a nap. She may show annoyance at being wet at certain times of the day.

Fifteen Months: Some children like to sit on the toilet and may pass urine or a bowel movement (BM); at other times they may resist. Their ability to retain urine and BMs has lengthened to a span of two or three hours. However, placing a child on the toilet may cause her to tense and withhold urine, and she may then release it as soon as she is removed from the toilet.

One to Two Years: Children attain nighttime bowel control.

Eighteen Months: A child can respond with a nod or shake of the head when asked if she wants to use the potty; this shows that she can now relate the words to the function. She may report accidents by pulling at her pants. Voluntary control may begin.

Twenty-one Months: A child reports accidents by pointing at her puddles. She usually tells you after wetting, but sometimes before.

She is pleased with her successes, but the number of daily urinations may start to increase and so the accidents may multiply.

Two Years: The child has better control and can verbalize her toilet needs fairly consistently. She may go to the bathroom and pull down her own pants. Bowel control may become established as the child attains voluntary control of the muscle that opens and closes to allow elimination.

Two and a Half Years: The child is able to hold urine in the bladder for as long as five hours. Two-thirds of children will be dry most of the time. Most are partially trained for daytime bladder control, and nighttime wetting may start to come under control.

Three Years: The child has few bowel or bladder accidents. She may be dry all night.

Four Years: Almost all children have complete daytime/nighttime bowel and bladder control.

Of course, these are just guidelines. Sometimes a child is not physically able to be completely trained "on schedule" because his or her neuromuscular system is not yet mature enough to perform the way you want it to. This is why it's important to remember that toilet training is not a discipline problem. There is no room for a drill sergeant in the bathroom.

Whenever you decide to help your daughter use the toilet and whatever method you choose to do that, your attitude toward the process is just as important as your daughter's. So keep these tips in mind:

- ☐ **Be matter-of-fact.** If you can stay unemotional about this developmental step you will give your daughter the message that the elimination process is a normal and natural one, a fact of daily living—not something supernaturally wonderful nor horrendously awful.

- ☐ **Be tolerant.** This will allow you to calmly bear events that are not at all what you had hoped or planned for. When your daughter sits on the potty for ten minutes with no results, for example, and then soils her diaper thirty seconds after you put it back on her, you'll need lots of tolerance to stay calm and supportive.

- ☐ **Be loving.** During the toilet-training period, show your child unfaltering love and affection. Make a point of offering lots of hugs and smiles. Let her know that if an accident happens, your arms will always be a safe place to run to.

LEARNING TO WIPE

You may have to wipe your daughter after a bowel movement for quite some time after she has become fully toilet trained. This is because:

- ☐ A toddler's arms are too short to fully reach the anal area.

- ☐ Toddlers lack the dexterity needed to wipe thoroughly.

☐ The consequences of an incomplete job are annoying for child and parent alike.

Some say girls are easier to toilet train and are ready sooner than boys. That may be, but in my family, one of my sons was far easier and was trained earlier than my daughter. But in the end, they all received their high school diplomas without the encumbrance of diapers.

Teaching a Little Girl to Behave

It's quite normal for all toddlers to seek out every conceivable danger and do exactly what they're told *not* to do. They have no self-control and no real concept of consequences. Unfortunately, all the scolding and disciplining in the world will not make them understand these things until they get a little older.

DISTRACT AND CONQUER

Because little girls find it so easy to get themselves into mischief, they need our help to stay out of trouble as they walk, run, stumble, and explore the world around them. At this age, the most effective way to keep your daughter out of trouble is to eliminate temptations. Keep her environment relatively free of no-no's—items such as stereos, jewelry, and cleaning supplies should be kept out of her reach. You will not stop a toddler's curiosity by saying, "No, don't," all day long. This is not discipline; it's systematic aggravation.

In situations where your daughter digs in her heels and is ready for a fight, try distraction before confrontation. Bring out a favorite toy, draw attention to a new activity, put on some dance music. You can also distract her with a hug and a kiss. Toddler upsets are often caused by frustration and are remedied with comfort and reassurance. Very often she'll gladly call a truce and move on without a fight.

SET LIMITS

While working to avoid trouble, you can also teach your daughter what she can and can't do by setting limits. Limits are rules that give structure to a toddler's world and help her feel secure. Consistent limits teach all children what is expected of them and how they should behave. Although toddlers may not appear to like the idea of rules, without them their world is too overwhelming and uncontrollable. After repeatedly testing you to see if you really mean what you say, your child will like the feeling of being able to count on certain things.

The limits you set should always be clear, consistent, and fair. Whenever you make a rule, test it against these factors:

- ☐ **Limits Should Be Clear:** A toddler's language skills are still weak, so your rules should not be too long or verbal. Simply say, "Don't pull my hair. It hurts me."

- ☐ **Limits Should Be Consistent:** If you say "no" this morning, and "yes" this afternoon to the same behavior, you can create a problem that will drive you crazy. It's like working a slot machine—your child quickly learns that if she keeps whining and crying, every so often the effort will pay off.

☐ **Limits should be fair:** If your daughter continually breaks every rule you set, you may have too many or inappropriate rules. A toddler's memory is just now getting into gear; it's impossible for your daughter to remember all the dos and don'ts of the world. So limit the number you expect her to remember to perhaps the two or three that really matter.

DIVORCE AND DISCIPLINE

After a divorce, the parent-child relationship often changes. A study reported in *American Psychologist* noted that the custodial parent (usually the mother) becomes stricter and more controlling, while the other parent becomes permissive and understanding, though less accessible. Both parents make fewer demands for children to mature, become less consistent in their discipline, and have more difficulty communicating with their children.

PRAISE AND PENALTIES

The two methods you can use to enforce your rules are praise and punishment. Many parents have found that praise is by far the more powerful enforcer because it gives kids the positive attention they crave.

However, the need for this attention is so strong right now that your daughter may learn to misbehave just to get it. That's why she'll act up as soon as you get on the phone—she knows she can't get your attention without making a scene. To her, negative attention is far better than no attention at all—but far better to give her positive attention. When you catch your daughter being good, stop and praise the effort. For example, "It's so nice to see you being good to the dog." If you do this often, you'll find you won't need to scold her quite so much for mistreating the dog.

Punishment, on the other hand, should be used far less frequently—even though that's the method of teaching good behavior most of us are more familiar with. We can all tell stories about discipline that begin, "When I was growing up . . ." But times have changed and because we now know that toddlers are unable to make any connection between their behavior and physical punishment, it's usually more effective to think of punishment as an opportunity for teaching a logical and age-appropriate consequence (that does not involve pain). For example, if your daughter hits another child, hitting her as punishment doesn't make sense and doesn't teach her what she did wrong. Instead, she should be told not to hit and then immediately removed from the play area. If she throws a tantrum out of frustration, she should be helped through the frustrating experience or ignored until she calms down (as explained a little later), not shaken or spanked.

An effective punishment for a toddler is a brief time-out to remove her from the center of attention. To get the most benefit from a time-out, choose a location that's away from the action to make your child feel somewhat isolated, but close enough for you to keep an eye on her. If she won't voluntarily go to the time-out chair, lead or carry her to the chair. Expect protests and ignore them. Make your daughter stay in the time-out chair for just a short time (one minute for each year of age is a good guideline). When the time is up, welcome your child back. Having to sit in a chair may not sound like a very impressive punishment, but remember, more than anything else, your child wants your attention. A time-out takes this away from her.

TANTRUM TIME

Setting limits and using praise and punishment wisely is a good start in teaching your daughter to behave. Unfortunately, it won't be enough to end tantrums completely. At this age, a child begins to develop a strong sense of self and wants more control over her environment. The conditions are right for power struggles: "I do it myself" or "Give me." When a toddler discovers that she can't do it herself and that she can't have everything she wants, the stage is set for a tantrum. Being tired, hungry, uncomfortable, frustrated, or in need of attention can all also prompt a child to have a tantrum. Growing up can sometimes be just too much for toddlers to bear.

So what should a parent do when a two-foot-tall demon child starts screaming and kicking? Most of us go with one of two common reactions: either give the child what she wants to quiet her down, or throw our own angry tantrum right back. In rational moments we know neither of these options is helpful, but when tempers flare it's hard to know what else to do (especially when the dramatic scene occurs in public—as it most often does).

I'm not saying it's easy, but the experts who have studied how to best control the behavior of a toddler say we should talk to our screaming meany firmly but calmly. Say, "You will not get what you want by crying and kicking your feet. When you calm down,

FAMILY RULES

When setting rules for your daughter, keep this list of don'ts in mind:

- Don't make the rules too long or too verbal.
- Don't change the rules; be consistent.
- Don't have too many rules.
- Don't overreact to tantrums with anger.
- Don't give in to tantrums or let your daughter have what she wants.
- Don't assume that because your daughter knows something is wrong that she will have the impulse control to resist doing it.

we'll talk about your problem." Then, they say, we should create some calming-down time by sending her to her room or to the time-out chair, or by ignoring her. This helps a child feel she has some control over the situation and it keeps her sense of self and competency intact. I have to admit, when I had the presence of mind and the fortitude to handle a tantrum this way, I got the best results and it makes perfect sense. Even a toddler will soon figure out that there's no point in putting on a show if there's nobody there to watch.

Teaching a toddler to behave and show self-control is not easy. It is a very slow and not-so-steady process. The key is to be patient and to never tire of repeating yourself. A toddler's memory is not very good. What you explained last week means nothing this week. Her impulsive nature makes it very difficult to stop misbehaving even when she does remember the rules. That's why you must select a few important rules and repeat them over and over to help your daughter eventually learn what's right and what's wrong in the world she lives in.

Water Safety

Most little girls love water. They can splash it, slap it, kick it, pour it, and push it all day long and keep coming back for more. Wobbling on their little toddler legs, they boldly enter the pool, lake, river, or tide without a second thought. And that's exactly what makes water play so scary for us as parents. We know the dangers and pray that our child will never be one of the heartbreaking statistics that make drowning one of the leading causes of death among youngsters. Toddlers are especially prone to water accidents because their arms and legs are small in proportion to their body and head, making them top-heavy. A toddler who falls down, even in shallow water, will have difficulty returning to a standing position—unless an adult is standing right there to help.

All my adult life I have been a lifeguard and swimming instructor, so I have a healthy fear of mixing toddlers and water. But I've also learned a few safety tips that have kept my kids safe and that may ease your own fears.

THE PROBLEM WITH "SWIMMING" LESSONS

Many experts have mixed feelings about swimming lessons for toddlers. There's no question that all kids should learn how to swim, but at this age, the primary purpose of the swim lessons should not be to teach swimming skills, but rather to introduce the basics of water comfort and safety. These early lessons can improve coordination skills, provide exercise for young, developing muscles, and set down a foundation for the later development of swimming skills. But they cannot make a toddler a good swimmer.

If you do enroll your daughter in a swimming class, be sure you understand its limitations. At this age, your daughter cannot learn to be responsible for herself in the water. So don't let a false sense of security lull you into thinking you can now actually read a magazine while your daughter plays in the water. Not yet!

Sanitary Swimming Ever notice that the water in kiddie pools is suspiciously warm? There's no doubt that all those little girls and boys are peeing in the pool. But urine generally doesn't spread illness. It's the bowel movements you have to worry about. Even in chlorinated pools, children in diapers can spread infection. So think twice before you allow your daughter to go in a kiddie pool full of diaper-wearing tots.

PLAY IT SAFE

While close supervision can prevent most water accidents, even the most attentive parents sometimes find themselves faced with a water emergency. You can reduce the likelihood of having a bad experience if you follow these simple rules:

- ☐ Don't expect floatation devices to keep your daughter's head above water. The majority of these devices, like tubes and water wings, are toys and are dangerous if used in any other way. Using these devices a child, can easily float into water over her head and then fall under. Even in shallow water, kids who fall down can actually be prevented from getting their heads above the water line because they're wearing these blow-up toys.

- ☐ Be especially cautious when your daughter is surrounded by older children. A toddler who is standing at the water's edge with older kids looks safe enough, but too often the little one is unintentionally knocked into the water. In the excitement of a game, no one may notice.

- ☐ Don't count on the lifeguard to watch your daughter. No matter how many guards are on duty, no one is assigned to watch your child. A lifeguard's job is to look out for major problems in a large group and keep the area safe to prevent water accidents; they are not babysitters.

WATER PLAY

The surest way to enjoy your time by the water is to get right in with your daughter. She loves to mimic you, so laugh a lot so she can see that you're having fun and praise her every effort. Here are a few simple water games that I've used in my classes to give very young children a foundation for learning basic swimming skills:

Ping-Pong Chase: Have your daughter blow at a floating Ping-Pong ball and chase it across the water. This game brings the child's face close to the water's surface and gets her ready for bubble blowing.

Ball Throw: Throw a ball up into the air and let it gently splash down in front of your daughter. The water will splash in her face, and when you laugh, she'll learn that water is fun.

Washboard: Hold your daughter up in the air with your hands under her armpits. Then lower her body down into the water just a little bit. Now lift her back up and down again. Each time you lower her, submerge a little more of her body until her chin touches the water. (Never throw a baby up into the air. Because her head is proportionally heavier and larger, there is danger of injury to the cervical area of the spine.)

Ring-Around-the-Rosy: This game is just as much fun in the water as it in on land. On the phrase, "We all fall down," your toddler might, at first, lower just her shoulders into the water. The next time, maybe her chin, and so on, until she plunges all the way under.

Use your imagination to make up lots of water games that you and your daughter can play together—*together* being the operative word. You'll have plenty of time during other summers for beach reading and sunbathing. For now, enjoy this special time when your child needs your undivided attention in and around the water.

Medical Care

One of the most important jobs of parenthood is keeping your child safe and healthy. During these toddler years, this job will keep you hopping. Your daughter's doctor will continue to monitor her growth and health at routine checkups where he or she will be particularly alert to any signs of food allergies or developmental delays. Here are some facts about the health of toddlers.

ROUTINE AT-HOME CARE

Introducing your daughter to table food is a fun and challenging experiment. It often takes a lot of time and patience to find foods that are good for her and that she'll actually eat. Good luck!

Eating Like a Big Girl: Your big girl is now ready to sit with the family and enjoy table food for three meals a day. Although your one-year-old may still be getting half or more of her daily calories from breast milk or formula, regular table food will help round out her diet.

Formula-fed and some breast-fed babies can now switch to cow's milk (unless there is some reason to suspect an allergy). Because babies need fat in their diets for development, most doctors recommend that they drink whole milk until they are two. Then, if their growth is stable and steady, they can switch to low-fat or non-fat milk.

Although your daughter is now at the family table, don't expect her to eat like an adult. She will usually eat only a small portion (and play with the rest). She may choose one favorite food and refuse to eat anything else (and that favorite food may change every few days). Most toddlers are quite finicky and often find new foods scary.

If you fight with your daughter over her food choices, you'll soon find that this is a battle you won't win. It's best to offer a variety of nutritious foods and then let her take the lead. If she refuses to eat anything but oatmeal cookies for a week, it won't hurt her (as my healthy daughter can attest to). If she'd rather snack on good foods throughout the day instead of sitting for three meals, that's also okay for now. Give her time to get used to good foods and a regular feeding schedule.

Excess weight: As your little girl begins to toddle around, you may notice that the "baby fat" on her cute little pudgy legs is no longer looking so cute. Once kids are up and about it gets easier to see that some one- and two-year-olds are already overweight and at risk for becoming a statistic in the epidemic of childhood obesity, which has doubled in the last twenty years. Doctors report an alarming rise in the number of toddlers showing early signs of weight-related health problems such as diabetes (insulin resistance) and heart disease, with their elevated blood fats (called triglycerides) and low levels of good HDL cholesterol.

As your daughter begins to eat table foods, now is the time to prevent health problems down the line due to excess weight. Before putting your daughter on a diet, talk to her doctor. Little growing bodies need an ample supply of protein, vitamins, and minerals that can be limited on low-fat diets or any of the popular adult diets. You can safely help your daughter meet her body's needs while staying in shape by following these guidelines:

☐ **Set a good example.** Your toddler loves to imitate you, so use that to your advantage. If you choose a piece of fruit for dessert rather than a bowl of ice cream, suddenly fruit will be your daughter's new favorite dessert, too.

☐ **Control portion sizes.** Rather than dish out food family style from bowls placed on the table, portion out servings on each family member's plate. Offer seconds only of lower-calorie, high-nutrient foods.

☐ **Offer lots of water.** Instead of high-sugar juice or soda, offer water or no-calorie fruit-flavored seltzer.

☐ **Limit fats and sweets.** Don't declare all fats and sweets off limits; you'll only make them more enticing. Instead, find ways to substitute—for example, an ice pop for ice cream, gelatin for pudding, macaroni with low-fat cheese for lasagna, a poached egg for scrambled egg, turkey for ham.

☐ **Limit TV time.** Sitting in front of the TV (and munching on junk foods) is a major reason for the rise in childhood obesity. Set a limit and then get your daughter up and moving.

☐ **Increase physical activity.** Toddlers rarely sit still, but often it's more fidgeting than moving. Make sure your daughter gets time every day for real physical activities like running and jumping for at least thirty minutes.

These suggestions are good for the whole family. So do not tease or embarrass your daughter by saying, "You're getting fat so you can't have ice cream." She is learning important lessons about health that will last a lifetime if they are taught with love and support.

CHOKING HAZARDS

Before the age of five, do not serve your daughter the following foods whole:

• hotdogs, especially when cut into circular pieces

• popcorn

• hard candies

• gum or jelly beans

• whole grapes

• raw vegetables such as carrots that are cut into circles

• spoonfuls of peanut butter or raw nuts

ROUTINE MEDICAL CHECKUPS

Your daughter's doctor will want to continue to monitor her health and physical development with regular checkups. Most doctors will schedule these visits at twelve, fifteen, eighteen, and twenty-four months.

The checkup will follow the same routine as earlier visits with a careful recording of weight, height, and head circumference. The doctor will again check her eyes, ears, nose, and throat, and will listen to the heart and lungs. He will feel the abdomen for enlarged organs and examine the genitalia for normal and healthy development. And inoculations will be given as needed.

The doctor will also tap your daughter's knees, shins, and elbows with a rubber hammer to check her jerking reflex. This tells him if her brain is sending messages properly down her spinal cord to the rest of her body.

The doctor will probably also ask your daughter to walk a straight line and jump up and down. This lets him evaluate balance and coordination.

He may also ask your daughter to touch her toes while he examines the alignment of the spinal cord. A curved spinal cord can indicate scoliosis.

When the exam is finished, be prepared with your list of questions. There's so much going on during these toddler years that it's hard to keep track of all your concerns, so write them down and then ask questions about them. This is a time when lots of parents wonder if their child is "on track." Is her language progressing as it should? Does she have good large and fine motor coordination? Is she really as smart as I think she is?!

COMMON HEALTH CONCERNS

There are two health topics that may especially concern you during the toddler years: The number of toddlers with food allergies is ever increasing—a good cause for concern as your daughter begins to eat "big people" food. And, of course, all parents want to know if their child is on track developmentally.

Food Allergies: We all know kids with food allergies—according to the Food and Drug Administration, up to 6 percent of children in the United States under the age of three suffer from some type of food allergy.

The allergy develops when the body's immune system mistakenly views food as harmful and produces antibodies to help fight off the invader. The antibodies release chemicals that trigger an allergic reaction minutes to hours after the food has been eaten.

Doctors can't predict which children will have these allergies and which ones won't, but there are various factors that place your daughter at risk. If you or your partner has a history of food allergies or suffers from other allergies or eczema, your child is more likely to develop allergic reactions to food (although some allergic children have no family history at all). Also, if your daughter has asthma, she is more likely to develop food allergies. And finally, children who are exposed at a very early age to foods that commonly trigger allergies are at increased risk.

A child can develop an allergy to almost any food, but the foods that most commonly trigger allergic reactions include:

☐ eggs   ☐ soy

☐ fish   ☐ tree nuts

☐ milk   ☐ citrus fruits and juices

☐ peanuts   ☐ wheat

☐ shellfish   ☐ corn

The symptoms of a food allergy range from a mild rash to life-threatening anaphylactic shock. If you suspect your daughter has had a bad reaction to food, tell her doctor. It's important to identify and avoid the offending food as soon as possible. Repeated exposures to an allergy trigger can make the allergic response more severe and more likely to be lifelong.

Of course, severe allergic reactions need immediate medical attention. You should call your doctor or 911 if you see these signs:

☐ red, itchy rash, or hives

☐ stomach cramps, vomiting, or diarrhea

☐ wheezing or shortness of breath

☐ feeling of light-headedness

☐ feeling of warmth, flushing, or tickling in the mouth

☐ severe sneezing

You can reduce the risk of food allergies by withholding common allergy triggers until your child's immune system has had time to mature enough to withstand the offending substance. Gradually introduce the common allergens listed earlier and watch for any signs of an allergic reaction. Wait until your daughter is two years old to introduce eggs, and hold off on introducing shellfish and peanuts until age three. Even if you've already given your daughter these products without a problem, it's best to avoid them in the future. Just because your child may have eaten peanut butter without an allergic reaction doesn't mean it still can't happen. Often the body reacts the second or third time a food is eaten.

If your daughter does develop a food allergy, your doctor can help. Although there is no cure for food allergies, there are medications to treat both minor and severe symptoms. The doctor will also advise you to steer clear of the offending food for a few years. Many children outgrow their allergies, provided that they are not regularly subjected to the food during early childhood.

Staying on Track: We all know we shouldn't compare our child to other children because each one is unique and will develop at his or her own rate. But . . . we all do. And we can't help but worry when our neighbor's child is walking at eleven months and our thirteen-month-old is still scooting around on her rear end. My own children taught me to be cautious when comparing one child to another. Joe was up and walking with confidence at ten months; Matt took his time and walked at fourteen months, while Colleen stood up and took off on her first birthday. These kinds of perfectly normal variations occur in many areas of development including motor, language, social, and thinking skills and are often no cause for concern.

But if you notice that your child is lagging behind other toddlers in her abilities, talk to her doctor. You'll get either reassurance that everything is just fine, or you'll get early intervention that can keep a small problem from becoming a much larger one. Early intervention is designed to identify and treat a delay in a child as early as possible because the sooner a developmentally delayed child gets proper help, the better her progress will be.

Today, the medical community is finding more and better ways to help babies, toddlers, and even young babies benefit from early help. These services range from early speech therapy or eyeglass prescriptions to a complete program that can involve physical and occupational therapy. If you're worried, don't wait to ask for an evaluation.

Physical Growth

While your daughter's developmental growth is moving ahead at an astonishing speed, her physical growth slows down after the first birthday. In the first year, she probably tripled her birth weight, but will now gain only between three and five pounds during her second year. Instead of rapid advances in weight and height, you'll now see changes in her appearance; her rounded belly and soft arms and legs will begin to trim down and become more muscular as she grows from a baby to a little girl.

KICKING MOTOR SKILLS INTO GEAR

Most kids are competent walkers by thirteen to nineteen months. And then, they quickly turn into speedsters who run, rather than walk, to every destination (or just for the pure joy of running). As your daughter inches closer to two, her large motor skills will continue to amaze. She'll climb stairs holding onto a banister with one hand while putting both feet on each step before moving on to the next. She will become extremely good at climbing and will be able to kick and throw a ball (although still rather clumsily).

Her fine motor skills are also developing, giving her greater control over her world. As you'll very quickly learn, the ability to use her thumb and fingers in a coordinated way lets her now twist knobs and dials, push levels, and open drawers.

Her improved fine motor skills dictate the kind of toys she now likes to play with. She can better grasp a crayon and will make actual drawings with recognizable shapes (especially circles). She can carefully stack blocks and with supervision can fold a sheet of paper, string large beads, manipulate snap toys, play with clay, and pound pegs. You can use these kinds of activities to get your daughter to sit still for a few minutes of quiet play before she jumps up to again practice those large motor skills of running and climbing.

TOYS FOR ACTIVE GIRLS

The best toys for this age group are ones that exercise large muscles (and expend all that energy). For outdoor play, give her toy ladders to climb, wagons to pull, and toy lawn mowers to push. Toys that she can ride on will also be a favorite and will help develop strength and large muscle coordination.

Emotional Development

Some say females are the more emotional of the sexes, but among toddlers, it's the little boys who cry more often and with more force than girls. But they cry for different reasons. Boys cry when things don't work as they should or when their routines are disrupted and, combined with kicking a door or hitting the wall, their tears help them voice their complaints.

Girls, on the other hand, are better at complaining with words (often very loudly) but cry more often than boys when they are hurt or need help. Some feel this is because girls are better able to use words to express their feelings, but are more dependent on adults for help and direction.

Whatever the reason, your little girl is bound to cry. It's part of being a person with feelings. When that happens, don't make light of those feelings by telling her, "Oh, that doesn't hurt," or "Be a big girl and don't cry." Instead, try to understand how she feels. The next time your daughter cries, try something like, "That must upset you very much. Let's see if a hug will make you feel better."

To give themselves emotional supports, some toddlers hang on to security items. It may be an old baby blanket, a tattered doll, or worn stuffed animal. My Colleen chose a particular bottle that she refused to give up. Anywhere she went, the bottle went, too.

If your daughter is dragging around a security blanket or a favorite stuffed animal (or a rather grimy bottle or cup), she has found a way to bolster her sense of emotional security, especially when you're not around. This, child experts say, is not a weakness;

IT'S ALL IN THE BRAIN

In general, female brains develop quicker than male brains. Brain development in infants is most obvious in the right hemisphere and gradually moves to the left. In females, the movement to the left starts earlier than in males, which gives females the early advantage in verbal skills. In most cases, little girls have larger vocabularies, are more verbally expressive, and will read sooner than little boys.

it is an early coping skill. If your child is attached to a "banky" or special "friend," don't discourage it or "lose" it when she's not looking (a real temptation when it becomes worn and tattered). She will give it up herself when it no longer serves an emotional need—although she may still want it nearby at bedtime for years to come.

Cognitive Development

Although little girls are just as intelligent as little boys, their cognitive development progresses at different pace. Your daughter has a better grasp of verbal skills than boys of the same age, but she may not be quite as good with spatial relationships. Her budding imagination will help her balance the two as she guides her toy cars through make-believe traffic and practices putting put her abstract thoughts into words.

THE GIFT OF GAB

The left hemisphere of the brain is far more active in females, making girls better at listening, communicating, and all language-based learning. This is probably why females have the reputation for being more talkative than males and men are described as "strong, silent" types.

At one year old, most babies say their first true word. (Although *mama* sounded like an attempt at your name, it was just a fun repetition of syllables.) Now you'll hear real words that refer to food (bottle, cookie), people (Mama, Dada, and the child's own name), and toys (ball, doll). At first, your daughter will use very basic word choices: she will say "dog" rather than "poodle." she will say "flower" rather than "tulip." And she will over-generalize: All men may be "Daddy," and all round toys are "ball."

Sometime between eighteen and twenty-four months, your daughter will have a vocabulary between fifty and five hundred words (that's quite a spread, because in the area of language development kids are all unique), and at some point will string her first sentence together. The thought in these sentences may not be profound (in fact it will probably be just two words long), but the accomplishment is a major advance in learning the language. So listen carefully.

After your daughter uses two words together to make a sentence, her language growth may explode. The sentences become longer, and she will soon add pronouns, plurals, and the past tenses of verbs. "See truck," becomes "I see truck." "I walk" becomes "I walked." These seemingly minor changes are giant steps forward.

This is also the time when your daughter's speech will mirror her growing independence. Most children quickly learn to say "No," "Mine," and "Me do it," and they practice these words all day long. Try not to interpret the "no" response as a sign of total negativity. Sometimes, it's just a fun word to say. (Interestingly, toddlers use the word *no* many months before they can use the word *yes*. But you probably already know that!)

Although language skills take giant steps forward between twelve and twenty-four months, there is still a lot to learn. You'll hear your daughter use pronouns and verb tenses quite creatively when she says, "Us go now," and "Truck comed." But these "mistakes" are all part of learning the language and are no cause to worry.

Your daughter's advanced language skills will continue to develop through the years, faster than her male friends. That's why girls move into reading readiness about two years earlier than boys. You can support and bolster these skills by trying some of these tips offered by child psychologist Charles Schaefer:

- ☐ **Fill in the blanks.** If your daughter says "Truck coming," you might reply, "Yes, a big truck is coming."

- ☐ **Add more information.** "That's a big delivery truck."

- ☐ **Use prompting to encourage vocabulary growth.** Say, "Here comes a big _____" and let your child fill in the blank.

- ☐ **Have conversations.** When you talk to your daughter, leave a pause, giving her a chance to respond.

- ☐ **Ask your daughter questions** (such as "What?" "Where?" "When?") that require more than a yes/no response.

☐ **Label things in the environment.** When you visit a park, talk about what you see: "Look at the see-saw. I see a white swan."

☐ **Play language games.** These include playing telephone, naming pictures in a magazine, and enjoying nursery rhymes and songs.

☐ **Simplify your speech pattern.** While your daughter is learning the basics, use simple sentences and speak a bit more slowly than you normally do.

☐ **Read!** Children learn about language by hearing it.

☐ **Avoid correcting grammar mistakes.** Simply repeat the thought correctly. If your child says, "Truck comed," you can say, "Yes, the truck came."

☐ **Don't let your daughter use pointing as her only method of communication.** When she points to the cookie jar, for example, say, "Do you want a cookie?" or "Can you say 'cookie'?"

☐ **Language development often moves two steps forward and one step back.** So don't be upset if your daughter "forgets" the words she knew yesterday.

AT HER OWN PACE

Try to resist the temptation to compare your daughter's verbal skills with other children. All children learn language at different rates and in different ways. Some say their first word at seven months; others wait until well into their second or third year. There is no definite timeline your child must follow. If your daughter is not saying single words at age eighteen months or has a vocabulary of less than ten words at twenty-four months, you should mention this to her doctor at her next checkup. But all speech development guidelines give only a general idea of what to expect.

OVERCOMING A DISADVANTAGE

Legos and Erector sets seem like gender-neutral toys to me, but apparently they're not. Boys show far more interest than girls in these kind of building toys for a very specific reason—boys have advanced development in certain areas of the right hemisphere of the brain that gives them better spatial abilities. This means they have a better grasp of shapes and forms, making them more adept at measuring, mechanical design, geography, and map reading.

And get this: it seems that this ability is inborn. Even male rats and monkeys are better at finding their way around than females. Studies have found that male rats tend to use geometric cues to find their way in a maze, while the females less successfully use landmark cues. Other researchers working with monkeys have found similar results with spatial tasks that require them to solve problems by rotating cubes. These studies and many others like them indicate that male superiority in spatial skills is found among all mammals (and, I'm guessing, in part explains why males hate to ask for directions).

To balance this seemingly inborn disadvantage for your daughter, add some spatial development games to keep her ability to manipulate shapes and forms from falling too far behind the boys. When little girls avoid building blocks and construction sets, which would improve their spatial skills, some teachers have found that they can increase their interest by adding a social aspect—little toy people! Encourage your daughter to build a house for the mommy and daddy, or a boat for the fisherman, and so on. The areas of the brain that control the understanding of spatial relationships can be strengthened with practice.

LEARNING TO PRETEND

At breakfast she is a dog trainer. By lunch, an astronaut. And after dinner, she's riding her horse off into the sunset. Don't you just love the imagination of little girls?

At this age, children are very imaginative—but they are not born that way. The ability to pretend is a mental skill that develops slowly at the same time a child begins to speak (usually between twelve and eighteen months).

The first signs of your daughter's imagination will be fleeting: lifting a toy cup to her mouth or a toy telephone to her ear. But soon, she'll be feeding her teddy bear and sitting inside a cardboard "house" with glee. By her second birthday, she'll be mimicking your every move while pretending to clean the house, drive a car, or unsteadily clomp around in high heels.

These imaginary moments are more than just pretend fun. The growth of a child's imagination moves her though many important development processes. For starters, pretend play lets your daughter explore her emotions. She can express anger by hitting a doll rather than a playmate. She can cope with fear by making her stuffed animal cry, rather than herself. She may practice love and tenderness by hugging and rocking a doll. And you may catch her working through her emerging understanding of right and wrong by scolding her stuffed rabbit.

Pretend play can also improve her language skills. Language uses words to represent real-life objects. So when your daughter makes a shoebox represent a car, she is developing the ability to think in terms of signs and symbols. Knowing how symbols work is a key factor in learning letters and numbers later on.

The list of benefits from pretend play is quite long. In research I once did for an article on children's imaginations, I found studies showing that pretending can enhance a child's self-awareness, self-confidence, and self-control. It has also been found to have a positive influence on a child's memory, language skills, and role-taking abilities. That's a lot of benefit from child's play.

Here are a few ideas that will help you encourage this wonderful gift of childhood:

☐ **Give your daughter toys that mimic the real world.** These include toy kitchen utensils, tools, garden equipment, and dolls.

☐ **Resist the temptation to substitute real for imaginary.** If your daughter is pushing a box around pretending it is a car, don't replace it with a toy car. If she uses a banana for a phone, go along with her without pointing out, "That's not really a telephone."

☐ **Hold back, even when you can do it better.** You may know how to play house better than your daughter, but let her work it out for herself.

☐ **Don't correct your daughter's "mistakes."** If she colors a picture of an elephant pink, purple, and orange, there's no need to point out that these animals are really gray.

☐ **Let her take the lead.** If your daughter wants to play school, let her decide who will be the teacher. If she wants to play dress-up, let her choose her outfit.

☐ **Get her out into the real world.** A dump truck or plastic farm animal can't spark imaginative play if your daughter has never seen a construction site or a farm.

IN THE TOY BOX

Those expensive toys that claim to make your daughter smarter are a waste of good money. That's the opinion of the child development experts I've spoken to. This is an age when children learn by imitating, by experimenting, and by doing.

Fill up the toy box with classic learning tools. These include blocks, dump trucks, stuffed animals, and objects that imitate "real life" such as toy hammers, play food, and miniature lawn mowers and doll carriages. Simple problem-solving toys such as shape sorters and nesting cups are also favorites at this age as kids learn how things fit together.

After eighteen months, creative toys will be a hit. Stock up on Play-Doh, crayons, and finger paints. And throw in toys that let your daughter exercise her imagination: dress-up clothes, action and animal figures, dolls, and stuffed animals.

Social Development

Most toddlers are very social little people. They love to be out and about and are very happy to be with playmates their own age. However, they are quite short on social graces and their behavior is naturally self-centered. She views the world according to her own wants and needs, so don't expect her to share or consider other people's feelings before she acts. Because she still hasn't formed a clear boundary between herself and the outside world, she sees all property as an extension of herself. To her the word *sharing* means "It's mine." This is why true friendships are very rare at this age. But this is the time when the foundation for friendships, peer relationships, and cooperative play is established—with your help.

FIRST FRIENDSHIPS

It isn't an uncommon scene: One toddler walks up to another, grabs away the toy, pushes the other child to the ground, and calmly walks away. What looks to some like an unfeeling act of a bully is really just another typical day in the life of a toddler.

Whether your daughter is the silent, play-by-myself type, or the everything-here-is-mine-so-stay-out-of-my-way type, she needs lots of opportunities to interact with other toddlers to learn how the give-and-take of friendship works. If your daughter is not already in a nursery school setting where she has probably learned to fend for herself, play dates are a good way to introduce and practice social skills.

Putting a bunch of toddlers together in one room is a setup for disaster if you don't plan ahead. More than once, I opened my door to toddling neighborhood kids and quickly found myself in the midst of crying children and broken toys. I soon learned to get organized.

In the beginning, it's a good idea to limit the number of playmates. One or two friends are plenty. And it's also a good idea to invite the child's parent to stay too if he or she has the time. Many children this age still want their parents nearby. Their presence raises the comfort level and reduces emotional meltdowns.

Playtime will go more smoothly (although never completely without upset) if you think ahead about the toys you'll offer:

☐ Beforehand, allow your daughter to put away treasured toys that cannot be shared. Children have a right to a sense of ownership.

☐ Select toys for sharing that you have duplicates of: dolls, trucks, coloring books, blocks, stuffed animals, and the like.

☐ Plan games and activities that can be played side by side. Rather than put all the blocks (or whatever) into one large pile for sharing, offer each child her own set. This will cut down on those conflicts of ownership.

Even with advance planning, kids will fight over toys. When this happens, wait a few moments before stepping in to resolve the dispute. The experience of pushing and pulling until someone wins the toy is often the first stage of leaning how to negotiate. If it looks like the battle is going to escalate out of hand or someone is going to get hurt, it's time to distract the combatants. Bring out a new toy or change the activity. If your daughter can't be distracted, don't punish her for not playing nicely. Instead, remove her from the fun for a few minutes so she can calm down and then go back and let her try again.

If you step in before the fight gets out of hand, you can sometimes introduce the idea of sharing. It won't work if you say, "You must share!" or "You shouldn't grab toys away from another child." Given her level of cognitive development, your daughter won't understand why she shouldn't take a toy she wants—it'll go in one ear and out the other. Instead, first acknowledge her feelings, then make a suggestion: "I see you want that ball all to yourself. When you're finished, will you give it to Ken?" This kind of dialogue introduces both children to the idea of taking turns in a way that does not shame them. This won't always have a happy ending, but if you continually put your child's feelings into words for her, you'll be surprised how often she will rise to the occasion.

When the children seem especially calm and happy, you can use this time of peace to teach them how to take turns by playing simple games. Have each child take a turn:

☐ Hiding and finding a ball under a blanket.

☐ Rolling a ball back and forth (to illustrate the notion that what you share eventually comes back).

☐ Putting blocks into a pail and dumping them out.

☐ Stacking three blocks.

Our kids don't need our help to learn how to play. But they do need our help to learn how to play with others. At this age, give them lots of social opportunities to try, fail, and then try again.

IMAGINARY FRIENDS

When other kids aren't around to amuse your daughter, she may surprise you by inventing her own imaginary playmate. I clearly remember when I learned about Colleen's friend "Bobby." One day she was sitting on the bottom step of the stairs. After a while, I asked "What are you doing?" "Waiting for Bobby," she said matter-of-factly. Bobby? "Who's Bobby?" I asked. "My friend," she replied and continued to sit patiently. I'm not sure if Bobby ever showed up that day, but he did occasionally pop up in her conversations for the next few months.

When I explored the world of imaginary friends, I was surprised to find how common they are. In his book *Human Development*, researcher Craig notes that as many as 65 percent of youngsters have imaginary friends and the creation of such friends is associated with positive characteristics. For example, in comparison with children who don't have imaginary companions, those who do are more sociable, are less shy, have more real friends, are more creative, and participate in more family activities. Imaginary companions also seem to help children learn social skills and practice conversations. In fact, one researcher found that they are powerful predictors that children will play happily in nursery school and will be cooperative and friendly with peers and adults.

So, there you have it. If your daughter begins to talk to thin air, or even ask for a second sandwich for her invisible friend, don't get alarmed. Apparently, it's a good thing!

Learning How To Be a Girl

Your daughter won't be quite sure if she is a girl or a boy until she's about three years old, but already she is learning a lot about gender roles—what it means to be a male or female in a particular society. Although gender roles in America have become more flexible over the last fifty years, most of us still have strong gender expectations for our children. A large chunk of our society expects boys to wear pants, get dirty, play tough, and not cry. Girls are expected to wear dresses (at least sometimes), play with dolls, stay clean, and be kind and quiet.

There are reasons for these expectations and some of them actually make sense. The roles assigned to males and females help children understand their gender identity. As they learn that they are girls, they want to know, what does that mean? They look around for ways to fit in and be accepted. Child-development experts have seen how little boys who prefer to play dress-up learn rather quickly to pretend they like football so they are not teased and put down by the other boys. Meanwhile, girls who play rough or with cars and trucks are often ridiculed or shunned. This awareness that girls do things differently than boys is tied in to the healthy process of self-discovery.

There is a down side to this realization, however. Too many in our society tend to view gender roles as inflexible, either-or barriers. You either are the man who is tough and strong, or you are the female who is weak and fragile. We see the "opposite" sex as having to be opposite: If girls are smart, boys must be dumb. If boys are active, girls must be calm. This kind of black-or-white thinking pits the sexes against each other at a very early age. It is not uncommon for a preschool male to refuse to play with a classmate simply because "she's a girl!" This is when you'll hear little girls quite confidently declare, "Boys are stupid."

This division of the sexes also limits life options. Although girls have far more flexibility than boys in exploring nontraditional female activities and careers, some still risk isolation and ridicule for their choices. And so they hide their more "masculine" ambitions. Too many girls still learn that being pretty is more important than being smart. They learn that being quiet is more "ladylike" than speaking up. And they still think that only men can be president of the United States. These lessons keep many girls from reaching their full potential.

We may notice these gender differences more in older children, but long before they even know they are male or female, toddlers gravitate toward stereotypically male or female toys. To me, the most astonishing thing about this is the speed with which children learn these stereotypical roles.

I made a conscious effort to raise my children in a gender-neutral environment where any role (tough, soft, dirty, or clean) was accepted. I filled our backyard with toys for exploring all facets of life on an equal basis. That's why I was so surprised when I looked out the window one Saturday morning and saw my two-year-old son pushing the toy lawn mower around the yard, while our neighbor's two-year-old daughter pushed the toy baby carriage. Where did they learn this stuff?

Apparently, kids pick up cues about the sexes very early and very rapidly. To test how toddlers connect gender with particular activities, future roles, and personality traits, researchers tried an interesting experiment. Given the two-year-olds' level of verbal skills, researchers taught the young children to point to pictures of "Lisa" or "Michael" to indicate their responses. They found that the children thought that Lisa liked to play with dolls, liked to clean house and cook dinner, talked a lot, and never hit, while Michael liked to play with cars and build things, liked to fight, and was loud, naughty, and made girls cry. They thought that Lisa would grow up to clean the house and be a nurse or teacher, while Michael would grow up to mow the grass and be the boss. Unbelievable!

SCIENCE SAYS

Researchers found that infants twelve to eighteen months old looked longer at photographs of babies of their own sex than at those of the other sex. Another study also found that infants looked longer at photograph of a same-sex child as long as the child was dressed in sex-typical clothing. Babies became confused when the other child was cross-dressed, suggesting that babies relied on clothing cues to determine the other child's gender.

WHY GIRLS ACT LIKE GIRLS

Do girls act like "girls" because they're hardwired at birth that way or because they learn female behavior from the world they live in? Nobody really knows for sure because there are strong arguments on both sides.

There are some scientists who believe that this early grasp of gender roles is inborn and caused by differences in the brain created by hormones in the womb. Males are exposed to higher levels of androgens, and females to higher levels of estrogens. Some of this gender study is based on interesting research done with opposite sex twins who naturally share the androgen and estrogen hormones. In these cases, the male tends to have more feminine attributes (lower in activeness, loudness, confidence, intensity, and selfishness) than his male peers, and the female twin shows higher masculine attributes (better spatial and mathematical abilities and increased dominance and sensation-seeking behavior) than her female peers. Researchers believe these results are due to the fact that androgen and estrogen hormones transfer from one fetus to another. This finding supports those who believe that at least some male-female differences are the result of hormone exposure in the womb and not the result of social conditioning alone.

Yet no one doubts that even if male/female behavior traits are inborn, the world a child lives in still has a mighty strong influence. Maggie Butterfield, director of community education at Children's Health Education Center at Children's Hospital of Wisconsin, says that there is no doubt that as parents we are the ultimate role models for our children. The way that we act our part as a male or female will be imitated by our children—for both good and bad. "If mom does all the indoor work and Dad does all the outdoor work," says Butterfield, "then our children will associate male behavior with the harder grunt work and females with the indoor caretaking work. So you might see more young girls playing 'house' while boys play construction worker.

"Of course, children will cross over these lines in their play because today they have more adult models who give them more options to imitate. One mom recently told me that her little girl packed up her backpack and said that she was going to the office. This mom worked outside the home and gave her daughter a nontraditional model to imitate."

Still, even high-level corporate moms and stay-at-home dads scratch their heads in wonder when they see their children play in stereotypical gender roles. The fact is, say many child development experts, that these moms and dads are probably not as neutral in their encouragement of crossing gender lines as they think. Children learn, not only by the type of toys they play with, but also through the reaction of others when they play with it. Buying a daughter a truck is not the same thing as smiling at her when she plays with it. Very often, children will receive more positive rewards for doing gender-typical things, and this encourages them to repeat those behaviors.

In one study that is very interesting but not really surprising, researchers Fagot and Hagan found that one-year-old girls and boys did not seem to care what toys they played with. Their play included dolls, puppets, and soft toys as well as trucks, cars, and blocks. However, when parents began to react more favorably to gender-typical toys during the second year, the children became more stereotypical in their choices. The boys, for example, received more positive reactions than girls for playing with transportation and building toys. The parents showed more interest and enthusiasm when joining in to play with toys that were more gender-specific. They found that parents tolerated some cross-gender play, but their positive reactions to such play declined steadily from about eighteen months on and declined faster for boys than girls.

Researchers have found that parents influence gender roles through toys in many subtle ways. When playing with their child at home, parents tend to reach first for gender-typical toys even when the child actually owns masculine, feminine, and neutral toys. They also play less enthusiastically with gender-atypical toys. In one study, parents were given a series of boxes that contained boys' and girls' toys, such as trucks, baby dolls, blocks, and a kitchen set. The parents' job was to open each box and get the child to play with the toy for several minutes. But the parents showed considerably less interest and excitement when introducing the gender-atypical toys and the children were more likely to reject them. Other researchers have found that parents have little need to monitor children's toy choices after the toddler period because by that time the lesson has been well learned.

Parents aren't the only ones who influence a child's view of gender roles. Children in daycare, for example, are likely to spend long hours in the care of a female. The role model here is the nurturing, caring woman. After spending weeks and months in this environment, it's unlikely that a little girl will say she wants to be a banker, or that a little boy will say he wants to be a teacher.

Playmates, too, are bound to influence gender ideas. In fact, author Susan Gilbert says in her book *A Field Guide to Boys and Girls*, that where attitudes about gender are concerned, playmates seem more influential than parents. She mentions an interesting study in which researchers observed groups of toddlers and preschoolers and found that boys were far more strict in their gender boundaries than girls. They found that the boys punished other boys by ignoring or teasing them for playing housekeeping, drawing, or engaging in other quiet activities. But the girls laughed, cheered, or joined in when the other girls played with trucks or acted rambunctious. Other researchers found that if a boy picked up a feminine toy, the other boys would make fun of him and, in some cases, even hit him. But when a girl played with a masculine toy, the other girls usually ignored her—not as directly critical, but still not the response kids want from their playmates.

Health educator Maggie Butterfield reminds us: "As parents, we can't assume that we are the only adults affecting our children's idea of gender. The child's grandparents, siblings, aunts, uncles, child-care workers, babysitters, and playmates, all play a role. This is especially true in families where both parents work long hours outside the home." No matter how careful you are to encourage your daughter's assertive and forceful side, you can be sure that everyone your child spends significant time with will also have an influence—and often that influence may encourage age-old stereotypes.

TEACHING GIRLS TO BE DEPENDENT

The way that parents, caregivers, and playmates react to girls teaches them a lot about how to be female. One of those things is how to be less independent than boys. Over and over child development experts have watched parents comfort their daughters who are fearful or sad by holding them close and soothing them, while they've watched parents comfort their sons with a quick hug and an encouraging push to "get back out there." While boys are encouraged to play independently, girls are given more one-on-one attention. When a girl follows her mother around all day, she's "cute and loving." When a boy does the same, he's a "pest and a baby." It is the boys who are expected to play independently, to solve their own problems, and fight their own battles. And so they do. Girls, on the other hand, often get the message that they should stick close to Mom and Dad.

And apparently they get the message. Researchers studying children's behavior found that when mothers placed their thirteen-month-old babies in an unfamiliar room filled with toys to play with, the girls spent more time near their mother, came back to her more frequently, and maintained contact more continuously through touching, glancing, and talking. Boys were more likely to go farther from their mother, perhaps even to the farthest side of the room, to spend less time close to her, and to check in with her less frequently.

So why do parents encourage this dependence in their girls? I have to wonder if we're biologically programmed to do this given that even rhesus monkey mothers tend to reject their sons earlier than their daughters and force the young males to establish their own independence!

Whether by social habit or inborn instinct I can see that there are disadvantages to raising a dependent little girl. But from my point of view as a parent, there is also an up side: Little girls are more easy to discipline than little boys. People in the know say there's no doubt that girls, far more often than little boys, stop misbehaving when the mother says "no" without having to be told twice. There is a theory that says this is because little boys are so starved for attention (since they are left alone to be independent so often) that they devise mischievous ways to get their parents' full attention. This explains why so many parents insist that raising girls is far easier than raising boys (not discounting the many little girls out there who also drive their parents crazy!).

BUSTING THE STEREOTYPE

After reading all this information about how toddlers learn how to be a girl or a boy, my bottom line question is this: Is it a bad thing when toddlers learn stereotypical gender roles? It seems that the answer is a definite yes and no. "It's a bad thing," says Butterfield, "only when we try to determine that there is only one role our children can play. Our job is to expose our children to a variety of things that they have the capacity to do and to be successful at. Some of these are traditional roles and some are not."

To do this for our children, we have to make a conscious effort and be aware that everything we do is being carefully watched and analyzed. (Not too much pressure!) Here are a few easy tips for giving our kids a broad, accepting view of what it means to be male and female:

☐ **Recognize the modeling you do.** When it comes to gender development, the old adage is true: It's not what you say, it's what you do that counts. Let your children see you sharing household tasks such as washing dishes, mowing the lawn, making repairs, and shopping for food so she does not assume that some jobs are done only by men and others only by women.

☐ **Expose your daughter to adults in nontraditional occupations.** Let her see a male nursery school teacher and a female doctor.

☐ **Monitor TV shows.** When you see a show that uses gender stereotypes, either turn it off or play a game of retelling the story placing the characters in different and varied gender roles.

☐ **Point out the biology of the sexes.** While bathing your daughter, name her vagina and tell her that only girls have a vagina—boys do not. (Your daughter would not be the first to then ask everyone she sees if he or she has a vagina and if she could see it!)

Learning how to be a girl takes time; it is a subtle back-and-forth dance between inborn tendencies and learned beliefs. It is remarkable to me that the gender beliefs picked up in these very early years can last a lifetime. So while it might be cute to hear a two-year-old say that only mommies can wash clothes, think how that same sentiment will sound when your daughter becomes a wife!

Growing Up Fast

As your daughter moves past eighteen months, you'll see that she's left babyhood behind in the dust. It's now full-speed ahead to the preschool years and beyond, along with all the excitement and adventures you will share together as your little girl ultimately begins growing into a beautiful woman.

MY BABY GIRL

"The best thing about having a daughter is that she is my shopping buddy. My two-and-a-half-year-old wakes up in the morning and right away wants to go shopping. I love it!"

—Elizabeth Elia
family dentist and
mother of one little girl

"Girls are so compassionate. My grandfather passed away recently, and my two-year-old daughter looked me in the eyes and kept saying, 'Mommy, don't cry. It's okay.' She can bring a smile to my face even during the worst of times."

—Cassandra Tiensivu

Epilogue

By now you should have a good sense of what adventures await you and your daughter during the first eighteen months of her life. You've also received plenty of advice and guidance on how to make the most of this very special time—always keeping in mind the many factors that make little girls different from little boys.

Learning about these differences has helped me to better understand my own daughter, and I hope the information will be useful to you as well. I now know why it was foolish to compare my quiet and reserved daughter to her high-wire and action-packed brothers. She is what she is in large part because she is female. Realizing this has helped me better meet her needs and understand her feelings.

Of course, for every generalization, there are exceptions and nothing stated in this book is absolute for all children. But knowing what "many" and "most" girls are like based on their body chemistry and the way their brains are wired gives us insights that I believe will help us all to be better parents.

In closing, I'd like to tell you how my daughter has grown to be a young woman. Through the many stories about Colleen that I've shared with you throughout the book (far more than she probably thinks is a good idea!) I'm sure you've noticed that she has faced the typical ups and downs of childhood with a calm demeanor and optimistic outlook. While remaining a bit shy, she has grown to be an outstanding athlete and student. She is a kind person with many friends and a smile that still lights up my heart. Colleen is now in the processes of choosing a college and next year will leave home to begin the next stage of her development. The emotional pain I feel at the thought of living each day without her presence around me is indescribable. But I will always have a life full of wonderful memories, which I have been happy to share with you.

As you raise your daughter, keep in mind that childhood is a temporary state that goes by very quickly. It won't be long before you look back and wonder how that cute little bundle of giggles turned into such an accomplished young woman.

Acknowledgments

The author would like to acknowledge the following people for their help in the preparation of this book:

Armin Brott: Author of *The New Father: A Dad's Guide to the Toddler Years* (Abbeville Press, 1998).

Maggie Butterfield: Director of community education at Children's Health Education Center/Children's Hospital of Wisconsin.

Freddie Curtis: Director of fashion design and fashion merchandising programs Harcum College in Bryn Mawr, Pennsylvania.

Cleveland Kent Evans: American Name Society.

Alice Sterling Honig, Ph.D.: Professor emerita of child and family studies in the College of Human Services and Health Professions at Syracuse University and a Fellow of the American Psychological Association and the Society for Research in Child Development.

Susan Isaacs Kohl: Preschool director, Lafayette, California, and author of *The Best Things Parents Do* (Red Wheel/Weiser, 2004).

Mark Langos: Interior designer.

Claire Lerner, LCSW: Development specialist Zero to Three.

Stephen E. Muething, M.D.: Associate director of clinical services for the division of General Pediatrics at Cincinnati Children's Hospital Medical Center.

Maureen O'Brien, Ph.D.: Director of parenting and child development at The First Year in Avon, Massachusetts.

Kirk Kazanjian of Literary Productions for having the vision that started this project.

My thanks also to Carole Beal of the University of Massachusetts, Amherst, whose writing on gender development first sparked my interest in this fascinating subject. And to the authors of these two books, which were invaluable in my search for answers: Susan Gilbert: *A Field Guide to Boys and Girls* (HarperCollins, 2000) and Michael Gurian: *Boys and Girls Learn Differently!* (Jossey Bass, 2001).

And a special thanks to Marilyn Gallucio, director of Enchanted Garden Nursery School in Hawthorne, New Jersey, and to all the moms and dads who shared their thoughts about raising little boys and girls: Lisa Cannizzo, Elizabeth Elia, Shawn Elton, Kristen Garza, Kim Marone, Tina Marie, Dominick Martone, Lori Suliot, and Cassandra Tiensivu.

Appendix A

Birth to 36 months: Girls
Length-for-age and Weight-for-age percentiles

NAME _____

RECORD # _____

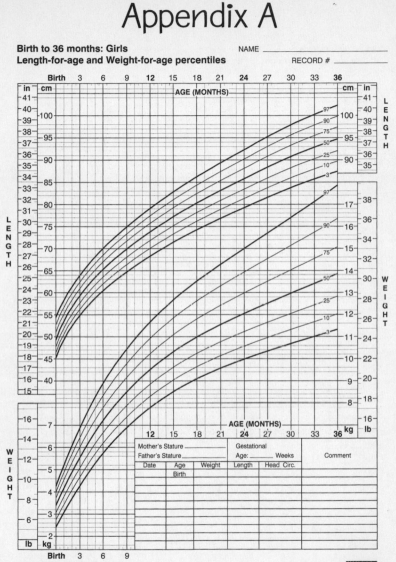

Published May 30, 2000 (modified 4/20/01).
SOURCE: Developed by the National Center for Health Statistics in collaboration with
the National Center for Chronic Disease Prevention and Health Promotion (2000).
http://www.cdc.gov/growthcharts

SAFER · HEALTHIER · PEOPLE™

2 to 20 years: Girls
Stature-for-age and Weight-for-age percentiles

NAME _____

RECORD # _____

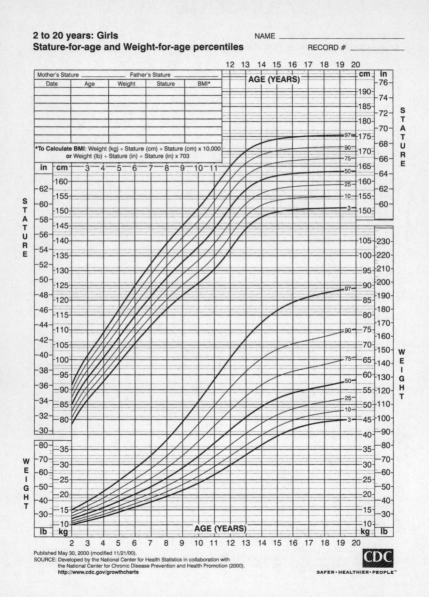

Mother's Stature _____ Father's Stature _____

Date	Age	Weight	Stature	BMI*

AGE (YEARS)

*To Calculate BMI: Weight (kg) ÷ Stature (cm) ÷ Stature (cm) x 10,000
or Weight (lb) ÷ Stature (in) ÷ Stature (in) x 703

Published May 30, 2000 (modified 11/21/00).
SOURCE: Developed by the National Center for Health Statistics in collaboration with
the National Center for Chronic Disease Prevention and Health Promotion (2000).
http://www.cdc.gov/growthcharts

CDC

SAFER・HEALTHIER・PEOPLE™

Sources

Chapter 1

Carole Beal, *Boys and Girls: The Development of Gender Roles* (New York: McGraw-Hill, 1994).

J. Train, *Remarkable Names of Real People* (Outlet Press, 1988), cited October 24, 2003, available at http://f2.org/humour/language/oddnames.html.

Elise Yong, "Oh, Baby, Give Me a Boy," *Record News*, September 24, 2003, Published in Hackensach, NJ sec. A, p. 12.

Chapter 2

Moss, Howard "Early Sex Differences and Mother-Infant Interaction," *Sex Differences in Behavior*, ed. R.C. Friedman, R.M. Richart, and R.L. van De Wiele (San Francisco, CA: John Wiley & Sons, 1974), p. 149–63.

Edward Tronick and Lauren Adamson, *Babies as People* (New York: Macmillan, 1980).

Chapter 3

Magnus Domellof, Bo Lonnerdal, Kathryn G. Dewey, Roberta J. Cohen, L. Landa Rivera, Olle Hernell, "Sex Differences in Iron Status During Infancy," *Pediatrics* 110 (2002): p. 545–552.

L. Tanner, "Premature Girls Have Better Growth Rate," *Pediatrics*, July 2003, cited January 2004, available at www.pediatrics.org.

Edward Tonick and John Cohn, "Infant-Mother Face-to-Face Interaction: Age and Gender Differences in Coordination and the Occurrence of Miscoordination," *Child Development* 60 (1989), p. 85–92.

Chapter 4

Carole Beal, *Boys and Girls: The Development of Gender Roles* (New York: McGraw-Hill, 1994).

P. A. Katz and S. Boswell, "Sex Role Development and the One-Child Family," *The Single-Child Family*, ed. T. Falbo (New York: Guilford Press, 1984), p. 63–116.

Lindsey Tanner, "TV May 'Rewire' Brains of Very Young Children," *The Record* April 5, 2004 sec. A, p. 7.

D. Tuller, "Poll Finds Even Babies Don't Get Enough Rest," *The New York Times*, March 30, 2004, sec. F, p. 5.

Chapter 5

Carole Beal, *Boys and Girls: The Development of Gender Roles*.

T. Bower, *Development in Infancy* 2nd ed. (San Francisco, CA: Freeman, 1982).

Jane Brody, "Fighting the Lessons Schools Teach on Fat," *The New York Times*, April 16, 2002, sec. F, p. 7.

Y. Caldera, A. Huston, and M. O'Brien, "Social Interactions and Play Patterns of Parents and Toddlers with Femine, Masculine, and Neutral Toys," *Child Development*, 60 (1989), p. 70–76.

G. J. Craig, *Human Development*, (Upper Saddle Ring, New Jersey: Prentice Hall, 1996).

J. Condry and S. Condry, "Sex Differences: A Study of the Eye of the Beholder," *Child Development* 47 (1976), p. 1417–1425.

L Ellis and L. Ebertz, *Males, Females, and Behavior*, (Westport, CT: Praeger, 1998).

B. Fagot and R. Hagan, "Observation of Parent Reactions to Sex-Stereotyped Behaviors: Age and Sex Effects," *Child Development* 62 (1991): p. 617–628.

Susan Gilbert, *A Field Guide to Boys and Girls*, (New York: HarperCollins, 2000).

Susan Goldberg and Michael Lewis, "Play Behavior in the One-Year-Old Infant: Early Sex Differences," *Child Development* 40 (1969), p. 21–31.

Melissa Healy, "Germ Warfare," *Record News*, April 6, 2004, sec. F, p. 1.

E. Hetherington, M. Stanley-Hagen, and E. Anderson, "Marital Transitions," *American Psychologist* 44 (1989), p. 303–312.

D. Kimura, *Sex and Cognition*, (Cambridge, MA: MIT Press, 1999).

D. Kuhn, S. Nahs, and L. Brucken, "Sex Role Concepts of Two- and Three-Year-Olds," *Child Development* 49 (1978), p. 445–451.

Charles Schaefer and Theresa DiGeronimo, *Toilet Training Without Tears*, (New York: Signet, 1997).

M. Siegal, "Are Sons and Daughters Treated More Differently by Fathers Than by Mothers?" *Developmental Review* 7 (1987), p. 183–209.

Index